Sew Fantasy Toys

Melanie McNeice

D&C
David and Charles

www.stitchcraftcreate.co.uk

Contents

Introduction   4

Materials & Equipment   6

Archie the Alien   8

Unidentified Flying Otis   12

Mili and Milo   18

Molly the Mermaid   24

Rufus the Robot   30

Yumi the Unicorn   38

Fifi the Fairy   44

Super Scotty   52

Dougal the Dragon   60

Princess Penelope   68

Stitching Techniques   76

Stuffing Techniques   78

Templates   79

About the Author   94

Acknowledgements   94

Suppliers   95

Index   95

Introduction

Ever since the beginning of time, people young and old have been fascinated by the imaginary world. Story telling, including some of our favourite fairy tales, has always included elements of fantasy, and there is no mistaking that we love being transported to a place where the imagination can run wild. Therefore it is with great excitement and anticipation of your enjoyment, that I introduce you to my realm of fantasy creatures.

This collection of exciting new toy patterns includes a selection of my favourite imaginary characters, designed to appeal to girls and boys of all ages. From an adventure-seeking mermaid who lives under the sea, to a big-eyed friendly alien and his sidekick UFO from a planet far across the galaxy, you are sure to find a friend here. Other characters just waiting to meet you include a less than perfect princess, a fashion-conscious fairy, a bedroom super hero, a couple of cheeky monsters, an action ready robot, an elusive unicorn and an eye-catching dragon.

The projects in this book have been given an experience rating and, as you work your way through the patterns, you can build up your toy-making skills. If you are unfamiliar with any steps, the Techniques sections are full of helpful tips, or you can visit my website for tutorials that offer step-by-step help.

Difficulty Levels

🧵 Great for beginners.

🧵 🧵 Perfect for the intermediate sewer with some experience.

🧵 🧵 🧵 Patterns suited to more experienced sewers.

I truly hope that whatever your fantasy creature of choice you enjoy exploring your toy-making talents with the patterns featured in this book, and that the resulting toys will bring somebody special many hours of imagination-filled play.

www.mellyandme.com

Materials & Equipment

Listed here is the essential equipment you will need for making the toys featured in this book.

Tracing paper or template plastic

These are the best materials for copying the toy templates and tracing them onto your selected fabrics. I recommend these products in particular because you can see your fabrics through them and therefore it is easier to ensure correct placement. The markings on the templates can also be easily transferred onto your paper or plastic and I recommend that you do this with a pencil or permanent marker.

Fabric markers

There are many different methods of marking your fabric and an array of products on the market. However, vanishing markers or tailor's chalk are the best options to avoid making permanent marks on your toys. A light grey lead pencil is a handy substitute. A pink pencil will also come in useful for marking rosy cheeks on the faces of some of your completed toys.

Rotary cutter, mat and ruler

These tools are designed to make the cutting of strips and squares a simple and accurate procedure. Although highly recommended, they are not essential items and you can use a tape measure, ruler and scissors instead.

Sewing scissors

These are frequently used when sewing any fabric project and I strongly recommend that you invest in good quality scissors to make your sewing experience more pleasurable and accurate. If you have both a large and a small pair of scissors you will be able to cover everything, from cutting out your fabrics to snipping seams and threads.

Sewing thread

It is essential when making toys that you use a good-quality polyester thread suitable for machine sewing. Strong, durable seams are required when stuffing toys, and if you use cotton threads, this will result in split seams. To achieve invisible seams, as far as is possible, match your thread colour to the colour of the fabrics you are working with.

Sewing machine

For strong, durable toys that withstand stuffing and boisterous play sessions, I recommend using a sewing machine for toy making. A basic sewing machine – one with a straight and zigzag stitch – is all you need, but if your machine does have blanket stitch, that will come in very useful for machine appliqué.

Hand-sewing needles

There is usually some hand sewing involved in making toys and therefore it is necessary to have some good quality hand-sewing needles. I recommend a size 10 embroidery needle for all hand sewing, and a selection of dollmaker's needles of different lengths are essential for button jointing or to attach items to stuffed toys, such as button eyes.

TIP

A seam ripper (quick unpick) is very useful for making a controlled slit for creating a stuffing gap as on Rufus the Robot.

NOTE
All measurements in this book are
given as height x width throughout.

Fabric and felt

For the toys in this collection I have used quilting cotton fabrics that are 100 per cent cotton and 100 per cent pure wool-felt. I recommend that you use these same materials to complete your toys if you want to achieve results like mine. Other fabrics may have more or less stretch and can create a very different result.

Fusible fleece

Some of the patterns require a lightweight fusible fleece in their construction. This is a white, lofty interfacing that is often used in bag construction, and it helps to give a thicker structure while retaining the softness that you will want for a toy. The one I buy is approximately 100cm (40in) wide.

Fusible webbing

This widely available iron-on material is used to adhere all appliqué pieces and facial features for example, to the toys. Be sure to check the manufacturer's instructions for your specific product before using.

Toy filling

Always choose a good quality polyester toy filling for stuffing. Some fillings can create lumps inside your toys, giving them a rough and uneven finish. To check a filling for quality, take a small handful of the filling and roll it gently into a ball between your palms. If the filling remains in a tight ball, it will create lumps, but if it springs back, it's ideal to use.

Turning and stuffing tools

A pair of tweezers makes turning through small limbs so very simple. A wooden skewer will come in very useful when turning and stuffing very small pieces (see Stuffing Techniques), but only use the blunt end of the stick – the pointed end is liable to break your seams. A round-ended wooden paintbrush makes a great double-sided turning/stuffing tool. The smooth handle of the paintbrush is perfect for turning your soft toy pieces and smoothing out the seams prior to stuffing, while the bristle end becomes the ideal stuffing tool with just a little modification. For more details on how to make the ideal paintbrush tool, see Stuffing Techniques.

Embroidery thread (floss)

You will need good quality six-strand embroidery thread (floss) for embroidering the toys' facial features and for hand appliqué.

Buttons

Round buttons in a variety of sizes make excellent toy eyes and are required when button jointing toy limbs (see Dougal the Dragon). However, if you are making these toys for a baby or small child, you should omit the buttons as they are a potential choking hazard: alternatives are provided in the steps.

Dressmaker's pins

Good quality pins are useful for keeping your fabric pieces together prior to stitching.

Iron and ironing board

Iron your fabric before transferring the templates onto it to get rid of any creases. An iron is also required for pressing seams, especially when joining fabric panels, and when using fusible fleece and webbing.

Archie the Alien

Finished size: 28cm (11in) tall

Ready to meet your very first alien?
Don't be nervous – this little green
extraterrestrial being truly does come
in peace. Topped off with an antenna
transmitter used to contact his friends
back home in a galaxy far, far away, he has
huge round eyes to take in the wonders of
our world. Having travelled all across the
universe, Archie the Alien has decided that
Earth is his favourite holiday destination!

Construction of this cute alien is quick and basic,
making him a perfect project for beginners or for
teaching a keen youngster to sew.

YOU WILL NEED

Note: Buttons should be omitted if making this toy
for a very small child.

* 38 x 30.5cm (15 x 12in) green spot print (head,
  arms, legs)
* 10 x 30.5cm (4 x 12in) blue space print fabric
  (body)
* 5 x 30.5cm (2 x 12in) red star print fabric
  (antenna)
* 7.5 x 15cm (3 x 6in) white wool felt (eyes)
* 7.5 x 15cm (3 x 6in) fusible web
* Six-strand embroidery thread (floss): black, white
* Two small black buttons for eyes
* Good quality polyester thread
* Good quality toy filling

Cutting Your Fabrics

Note: Trace the Alien templates (see Templates) onto tracing paper or template plastic, transferring all of the markings, and cut them out along the traced lines. When using these templates to trace the pattern pieces onto your fabric, do ensure that the marked grain line on the template matches the grain line of your fabric.

From your green spot print

Cut one strip measuring 16.5 x 30.5cm (6½ x 12in).

Cut one strip measuring 7.5 x 30.5cm (3 x 12in).

Fold the remaining fabric in half with right sides together; trace the arm template twice onto the folded fabric, but **do not** cut out (these will be sewn on the traced line).

Preparing to Start

1 Trace the eye circle twice onto the paper side of the fusible web and rough cut ou; fuse the eyes to the white wool felt and cut out along the traced lines.

2 Set your sewing machine to a small stitch length of approx 1.5 for stitching the toy and use a good-quality polyester thread for strong seams.

Making the Alien

Note: A 6mm (¼in) seam allowance is included in all pattern pieces unless advised otherwise. Read through all instructions before beginning to avoid surprises.

1 Take the strip of green spot print fabric measuring 16.5 x 30.5cm (6½ x 12in) and your red star print fabric strip. Place fabrics with right sides together, aligning along one long edge and stitch to create a panel (see Fig. 1). Press seam open.

Fig. 1

2 Fold your fabric panel in half width ways with right sides together so that the short edges meet and fabric seams meet evenly. Place the head template onto the folded fabric panel making sure that the marked antenna line matches up with the fabric seam. Trace around the template and cut the head out along the traced line to give you two head pieces.

3 Take your second strip of green spot print fabric and join it to the blue space-print fabric to make a second fabric panel (see Fig. 2). Press seam open.

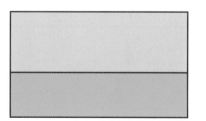

Fig. 2

4 Take this fabric panel and fold in half width ways, so that the short edges meet and right sides are together, and making sure that the fabrics and seam line are perfectly aligned. Place the body template onto the folded fabric panel making sure that the leg line matches up with the seam in the fabric. Trace around the template and then cut the body out along the traced line to give you two body pieces.

5 Take the remaining piece of folded green spot print fabric that has the arms traced onto it and, keeping the fabric folded, sew along the traced lines of the arms, leaving the straight ends unstitched as indicated by the broken line on the template. Cut out each arm approx 3–6mm (⅛– ¼in) outside your sewn lines, lightly snip the seam between the fingers. To turn the arms effortlessly, insert a pair of tweezers into the arm and pinch the sewn end, hold tight and pull through to the right side.

6 Firmly stuff the arms to the very ends with toy filling, leaving the last 2cm (¾in) unstuffed. Tack (baste) the open ends closed.

7 Take one of the body pieces and place it right side up on your work surface. Place the arms on top of the body aligning the raw edge of the arms with the raw edge of the neckline and positioning the arms approx 1.3cm (½in) in from the sides. Machine tack (baste) in position close to the raw edge (see Fig. 3).

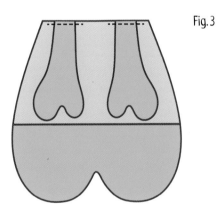

Fig. 3

8 Take one head piece and the body piece with arms and place on top of each other with right sides together so that they are aligned at the neckline. Pin in place, and then sew along the neckline. This is the joined front piece.

9 Take your remaining body and head pieces and place on top of each other with right sides together so that they are aligned at the neckline. Pin in place, and then sew along the neckline, leaving the middle section open for turning and stuffing as indicated by the broken line on the body template. This is the joined back piece.

10 Take your joined front and your joined back piece and place on top of each other, right sides together, and pin in place all the way around the outside edge making sure that the neckline seams meet evenly. Sew the body pieces together all the way around the pinned edge.

11 Turn the body right-side out through the neckline gap. Stuff firmly with toy filling. Ladder stitch the opening closed (see Stitching Techniques), stuffing in a little more as you go to avoid a dimple.

12 Take the white eye circles and fuse them in place on the face. Using two strands of white embroidery thread (floss), blanket stitch the eyes in place, sinking the knots to start and finish (see Stitching Techniques).

13 Mark the mouth onto the face (see template for position) and backstitch over the marked line using two strands of black embroidery thread (floss). Finally, sew on the two small black button eyes (or blanket stitch small black felt circles in place if making for a very young child).

Unidentified Flying Otis

Finished size: 15cm (6in) tall

Look who's just landed – it's Otis, our very friendly flying saucer. This is his first mission to Earth, where he is hoping to bump into Archie the Alien to find out all about his adventures on his voyage of intergalactic discovery. With bright flashing lights on his colourful saucer and a very winning smile, Otis brightens up the night sky, so you can't fail to spot him as he flies by.

Construction of Otis is basic so he is quick to make using small pieces of your favourite fun prints.

YOU WILL NEED

★ 25 x 20cm (10 x 8in) green spot print fabric (dome)
★ 20 x 20cm (8 x 8in) each of four contrasting print fabrics (saucer sides and base)
★ 20cm (8in) x full width lightweight fusible fleece
★ 7.5 x 15cm (3 x 6in) lime wool felt (saucer lights)
★ 5 x 10cm (2 x 4in) white wool felt (eyes)
★ 2.5 x 2.5cm (1 x 1in) black wool felt (eyes)
★ 60cm (24in) medium lime cotton ric-rac
★ 15 x 15cm (6 x 6in) fusible web
★ Six-strand embroidery thread (floss): black, white
★ Good quality polyester thread
★ Good quality toy filling

Cutting Your Fabrics

Note: Trace the UFO templates (see Templates) onto tracing paper or template plastic, transferring all of the markings, and cut them out along the traced lines. When using these templates to trace the pattern pieces onto your fabric, do ensure that the marked grain line on the template matches the grain line of your fabric.

From your green spot print

Trace the dome template twice onto folded fabric and cut out along the traced lines to give you four dome pieces.

From your four contrasting print fabrics

First, interface each piece with fusible fleece.

Trace the base template once and the saucer template twice onto the fleece side of each of your contrasting print fabric pieces and cut out along the traced lines.

Preparing to Start

1 Working on the paper side of the fusible web, trace the light circle eight times, the larger eye circle twice, and the smaller pupil circle twice, and rough cut out all the circles. Putting the larger eye circles aside for now, fuse the light circles to the lime wool felt and the pupils to the black wool felt, and cut out along the traced lines.

2 Set your sewing machine to a small stitch length of approx 1.5 for stitching the toy and use a good quality polyester thread for strong seams.

Making the UFO

Note: A 6mm (¼in) seam allowance is included in all pattern pieces unless advised otherwise. Read through all instructions before beginning to avoid surprises.

1 Take the eight fleece-backed saucer pieces and fuse a green light circle in the centre of each (see saucer template). Machine appliqué each circle in place by topstitching close to the edge.

2 Take two contrasting saucer pieces and place on top of each other with right sides together. Sew sew along one side edge to create your first quarter section (see Fig. 1). Press the seams open.

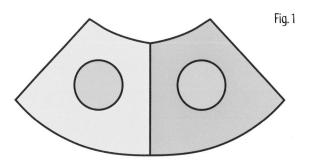

Fig. 1

3 Repeat step 2 with the remaining saucer pieces to complete the quarter sections that make up the sides of the saucer (see Fig. 2).

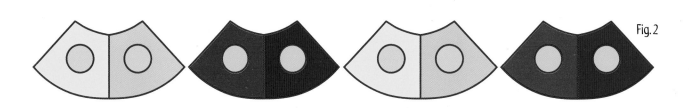

Fig. 2

4 Take one of the quarter side sections and one of the green spot print dome pieces and place on top of each other with right sides together so that the bottom edge of the dome piece aligns with the top edge of the quarter side section. Pin along the edge so that the dome piece is neatly centred on the quarter side section, and then sew along this seam (see Fig. 3). Repeat to join the remaining three quarter side sections to the remaining three dome pieces. You now have four joined dome/side sections.

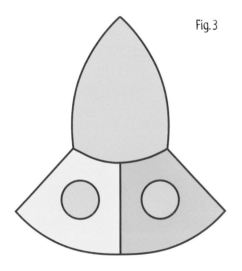

Fig. 3

5 Take two of your dome/side sections, making sure they are different colours, and place on top of each other with right sides together. Sew the two sections together along one side edge from the top point of the dome to the bottom corner of the side section. Snip into the seam. Repeat to join the remaining two dome/side sections so that the side colours run in the same order.

6 Take the two halves of your flying saucer (dome/ sides) and place on top of each other with right sides together. Sew the two halves together at each side to complete your flying saucer top, remembering to snip into the seams.

7 Now to make the flying saucer base. Being mindful of the final colour placement, take two of the fleece-backed base pieces, and place on top of each other with right sides together. Sew together along one straight edge only and press seams open to give you a half circle. Repeat with the remaining two base pieces to give you a second half circle.

8 Take the two half circles and place on top of each other with right sides together. Sew together along the straight edge leaving a 7cm (2¾in) gap in the middle for turning. Press seams open.

TIP

Snipping into the seams of the interfaced fabric, especially at the dome/saucer junctions, will allow more flexibility for turning and ensures a better shape.

9 Take your length of ric-rac and referring to Fig. 4, position this neatly around the outer edge of your base circle, right sides together. Machine tack (baste) into place, curving the raw ends of the ric-rac to the outside of your circle where they meet.

Fig. 4

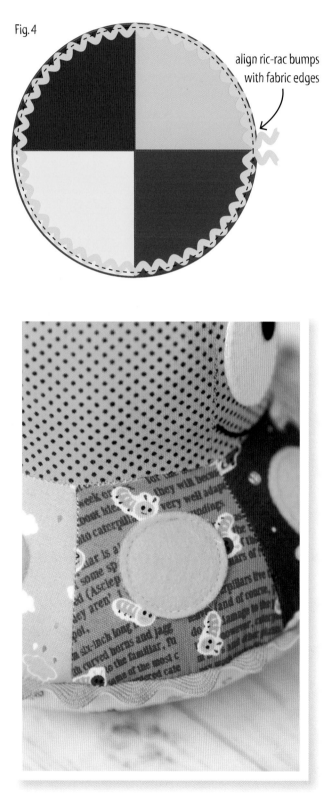

align ric-rac bumps with fabric edges

10 Take the flying saucer top and base and place them on top of each other with right sides together. Matching up the seams at the quarter points, pin and then sew together all the way around the outer edges of the circle. Trim all the layers of this seam allowance to approx 3mm (⅛in) to allow more flexibility, and then turn the flying saucer to the right side through the gap in the base.

11 Stuff the UFO very firmly with toy filling: stuff the dome section well first before continuing to stuff the saucer, making sure to fill out all of the curves and edges neatly – using the paintbrush tool will help (see Stuffing Techniques). Once fully stuffed, ladder stitch the opening closed (see Stitching Techniques), stuffing in a little more as you go to avoid a dimple.

12 Now to make the eyes. Fuse the small circles of black wool felt (pupils) onto your piece of white wool felt, ensuring there is enough room between to allow you to cut out the eye shapes. Machine appliqué the pupils in place by topstitching close to the edge.

13 Take your pieces of set-aside fusible web with the eye circles traced on and fuse them to the reverse of your white felt, using the stitching line of the pupils as a guide to positioning.

14 Cut the eyes out along the traced lines. Fuse the eyes in place on the dome referring to the photograph. Using two strands of white embroidery thread (floss), blanket stitch the eyes in place, sinking the knots to start and finish (see Stitching Techniques).

15 Mark the position of the mouth onto the toy and chain stitch along the marked line using two strands of black embroidery thread (floss) (see Stitching Techniques).

Mili and Milo

Finished size: 19cm (7½in) tall

Meet Mili and Milo, a pair of monster twins who are always ready to play. They love to hide under the bed or behind open wardrobe doors, ready to jump out at you. When they do, they are sure to bring a squeal of laughter rather than a yelp of alarm, for they are all about fun. With their big eyes and cuddle-ready arms, this cheeky duo will capture your heart.

Construction of these playful monsters is quick and basic – perfect for beginners or young sewers.

YOU WILL NEED
(FOR EACH MONSTER)

★ 25 x 46cm (10 x 18in) patterned fabric (body)

★ 15 x 15cm (6 x 6in) spot print fabric (arms)

★ 20cm (8in) jumbo ric-rac in colour to match

★ 10 x 12.5 cm (4 x 5in) wool felt in colour to match (face)

★ 10 x 10cm (4 x 4in) black wool felt (eyes)

★ 7.5 x 7.5cm (3 x 3in) white wool felt (face details)

★ 5 x 5cm (2 x 2in) pink wool felt (Mili's cheeks)

★ 12.5 x 20cm (5 x 8in) fusible web

★ Six-strand embroidery thread (floss): black

★ Good quality polyester thread

★ Good quality toy filling

Preparing to Start

Note: Trace the Monster templates (see Templates) onto tracing paper or template plastic, transferring all markings; cut out along the traced lines.

1 Trace the face, eyes and face details for your chosen monster onto the paper side of the fusible web and rough cut out. Fuse the cut out shapes to your relevant wool felt pieces, and then cut out along the traced lines.

2 Take the piece of spot print arm fabric and fold it in half with right sides together. Trace the arm template twice onto the folded fabric but **do not** cut out.

3 Set your sewing machine to a small stitch length of approx. 1.5 for stitching the toy and use a good quality polyester thread for strong seams.

Making the Monster

Note: A 6mm (¼in) seam allowance is included in all pattern pieces unless advised otherwise. Read through all instructions before beginning to avoid surprises.

1 Take your piece of patterned (body) fabric and fold in half width ways with right sides together (now measures 25 x 23cm/10 x 9in). Press the fabric to create a crease at the halfway mark. Unfold the fabric and lay it on your work surface with right side facing up. Take the felt face shape and fuse it in the centre of the right-hand side of your fabric (see Fig. 1). Machine appliqué the face in place with straight stitch very close to the edge.

Fig. 1

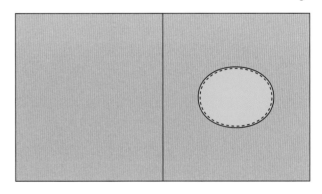

2 Take your remaining felt face shapes and refer to the templates and the detail photographs of each monster's face for where to position and the order in which to place, fuse and sew in place.

TIP

Change your sewing thread to black when stitching the black eye circles in place for a neater look.

3 Referring to the templates, mark any stitching lines (mouth, eyelashes, eyebrows, cheek spots) onto your chosen monster's face. Stitch along the marked lines using four strands of black embroidery thread (floss) and backstitch, with the exception of Milo's cheeks, which are worked with running stitch (see Stitching Techniques).

4 Refold the fabric panel with right sides together, so that the side with the back of the face appliqué stitching is facing you. Take the body template and place it on the fabric so that the marked face shape lines up with the face appliqué stitching. Trace around the template making sure to mark both the turning gap and the ric-rac gap (indicated by broken lines on the template). **Do not** cut out.

TIP

When fusing the monsters' facial details work from the bottom layers up, using the detail photographs of Mili and Milo as your guide.

5 Sew the body together on the traced line, leaving the marked turning and ric-rac gaps open. Cut out the body approx 6mm (¼in) outside your sewn and traced lines.

6 Take your length of jumbo ric-rac and position it neatly at the ric-rac gap along one side of the head. You want to fit three bumps of the ric-rac into the gap, curving the raw ends to the outside of your body shape (see Fig. 2). Sew the ric-rac in place by stitching the gap closed along the traced line. Trim any excess ric-rac.

Fig. 2

curve ends of ric-rac to
outside for neat finish

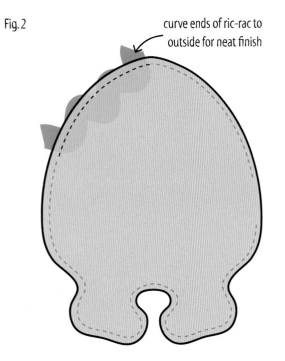

7 Before turning your monster right side out, snip into the angled seam allowance between its legs. Turn the body through the turning gap in the side, and then stuff very firmly with toy filling. Ladder stitch the opening closed (see Stitching Techniques) adding a little more stuffing as you go to avoid a dimple.

8 Take your folded piece of spot-print fabric with the arms traced onto it and, keeping the fabric folded, sew along the traced lines of the arms, leaving the straight ends unstitched as indicated by the broken line on the template. Cut out each arm approx 3–6mm (⅛– ¼in) outside your sewn lines, lightly snip the seam between the fingers, and turn the arms right side out.

9 Fold the raw ends of the turning gaps in on each arm by approx 6mm (¼in) and finger press in place. Stuff the arms firmly right to the folded ends.

10 Position an arm onto one side of your monster, referring to the photo as a guide to positioning. Hold the arm in place by pinning through the arm and into the body, much like a pin cushion. Using strong polyester thread, ladder stitch the arm in place (see Stitching Techniques: Attaching Parts): work the ladder stitch in a circle and go around at least twice to ensure a firm attachment. Repeat to sew on the second arm.

TIP
To add a finishing touch to Mili, why not ladder stitch a small flower embellishment to her head? Small felt or crochet flowers can be bought, or you could make your own.

23

Molly the Mermaid

Finished size: 28cm (11in) tall

Meet Molly the Mermaid, but you'll have to be quick as she will soon be off with a swish of her tail, seeking another adventure in her underwater world. Her favourite pastime is to scour the ocean floor, seeking the very brightest of starfish to decorate her hair. She is particularly proud of her latest find as it is the exact same shade of purple to match her lovely hair bunches.

Construction of Molly is quite basic but she will help you to build on beginner skills. She can be whipped up in no time and she can be customized to suit your preferences from skin tone to hair colour.

YOU WILL NEED

★ 25 x 30.5cm (10 x 12in) plain fabric (head front, body, arms)
★ 28 x 28cm (11 x 11in) green print fabric (tail, flippers)
★ 30 x 15cm (12 x 6in) aqua wool felt (head back, hair)
★ 5 x 12.5cm (2 x 5in) purple wool felt (stars)
★ 7.5 x 28cm (3 x 11in) lightweight fusible fleece
★ 15 x 20cm (6 x 8in) fusible web
★ Six-strand embroidery thread (floss): black, red
★ 120cm (47in) purple mini ric-rac (hair bunches)
★ 50cm (20in) narrow ribbon in colour to match
★ Pink pencil
★ Good quality polyester thread
★ Good quality toy filling

Cutting Your Fabrics

Note: Trace the Mermaid templates (see Templates) onto tracing paper or template plastic, transferring all the markings, and cut them out along the traced lines. When using these templates to trace the pattern pieces onto your fabric, do ensure that the marked grain line on the template matches the grain line of your fabric.

From your plain fabric

Cut one piece measuring 10 x 20cm (4 x 8in) for the arms.

Trace the head template once and the body template twice onto the remaining fabric and cut out along the traced lines.

From your green print fabric

Cut one piece measuring 7.5 x 28cm (3 x 11in) for the flippers.

Fold the remaining fabric in half with the right sides together. Trace the tail template once onto the folded fabric and cut out along the traced line to give you two tail pieces.

From your aqua wool felt

Trace the head template once onto one half of your felt and cut out along the traced line: this is the head back.

Preparing to Start

1 Interface the green print flippers fabric strip with the fusible fleece.

2 Trace the hair template once and the star template three times onto the paper side of the fusible web and rough cut out. Fuse the hair shape to your remaining aqua wool felt and the three stars to the purple wool felt, and cut out all the pieces along the traced lines.

3 Set your sewing machine to a small stitch length of approx 1.5 for stitching the toy and use a good-quality polyester thread for strong seams.

Making the Mermaid

Note: A 6mm (¼in) seam allowance is included in all pattern pieces unless advised otherwise. Read through all instructions before beginning to avoid surprises.

1 Take the plain fabric head piece and the aqua felt hair piece. Fuse the hair piece onto the right side of the head piece, making sure the pieces are neatly and evenly aligned. Referring to the photo, machine appliqué the hair piece into place along the face edge only using straight stitch worked very close to the edge of the felt.

2 Take one of the purple felt stars and fuse it onto the hair in your desired position. Machine appliqué into place.

3 Trace the eye and mouth markings onto Molly's face. Using two strands of black embroidery thread (floss), stitch the eyes with satin stitch then backstitch the eyelashes (see Stitching Techniques). Using two strands of red embroidery thread (floss), backstitch the mouth.

4 Take one of the plain fabric body pieces and the two remaining purple felt stars. Fuse the stars onto the body piece, positioning them approx 6mm (¼in) apart and 1.3cm (½in) down from the neckline, and machine appliqué into place (see Fig. 1). This is the body front.

Fig. 1

5 Take your folded piece of plain fabric with the arms traced onto it and, keeping the fabric folded, sew along the traced lines of the arms, leaving the straight ends unstitched as indicated by the broken line on the template. Cut out each arm approx 3–6mm (⅛–¼in) outside your sewn lines, and then turn right side out. Firmly stuff the arms with toy filling, leaving the last 2cm (¾in) unstuffed. Tack (baste) the open ends closed.

6 Take the body front (with stars) and place it right side up on your work surface. Place the arms on top of the body aligning the raw edge of the arms with the raw edge of the neckline and positioning the arms approx 1.3cm (½in) in from the sides. Machine tack (baste) in position close to the raw edge (see Fig. 2).

Fig. 2

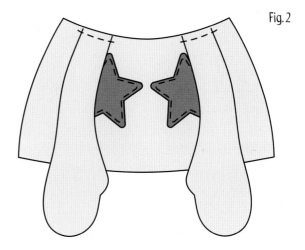

7 Take the head front and the body front and place these on top of each other with right sides together, making sure that they are aligned so that the centre of the body front neckline meets the centre of the bottom of the head; pin in place. Sew together along the neckline.

8 Take the joined front body/head piece and one of the green print tail pieces and place on top of each other, right sides together, so they are centrally aligned at the waistline; pin in place and sew together.

9 Take the remaining plain fabric body piece and the aqua felt head piece, and place them on top of each other with right sides together, aligning them at the neckline. Pin in place and then sew together along the neckline, leaving the middle section open for turning and stuffing as indicated by the broken line on the body template. This is the joined back body/head.

10 Take the remaining tail piece and joined back body/head and place them on top of each other with right sides together, so that they are aligned at the waistline. Pin in place, then sew together.

11 To make Molly's hair bunches, start by taking your length of ric-rac and cut it into 12 pieces measuring approx 10cm (4in) each. Take six of the ric-rac pieces and fold them in half; secure the raw ends together tightly with a small piece of tape to make a hair bunch (see Fig. 3). Make a second hair bunch with the remaining six lengths of ric-rac.

Fig. 3

sticky tape

12 Place the mermaid front right side up on your work surface. Position the ric-rac hair bunches on top, so that the taped ends of the bunches sit beyond the sides of the head front with the bunches pointing inwards towards the face (see Fig. 4 for positioning). Machine tack (baste) into place.

Fig. 4

13 Place the mermaid front and the mermaid back on top of each other with right sides together and pin in place. Sew all the way around the body, leaving the flipper gaps at the bottom of the tail unstitched as indicated by the broken lines on the tail template. **Do not** turn the body through just yet as the flippers must be added first.

14 Take the fleece-backed green print fabric strip and fold in half, right sides together. Trace the flipper template twice onto one side of the folded strip, flipping the template for the second tracing. Sew along the traced lines, leaving the straight ends unstitched as indicated by the broken line on the template. Cut out approx 3mm (⅛in) outside the sewn lines, turn each right side out and press.

15 Take the mermaid body and insert one of the flippers, raw edges first, through the turning gap on the back of the neckline, guiding the raw edge into one of the flipper gaps along the bottom edge of the tail. Making sure that the raw edge of the flipper aligns with the raw edge of the gap, and following the traced line of the body, sew the flipper in place. (Note: the flipper is inside the body.) Repeat for the second flipper in the remaining gap.

16 Turn the mermaid right side out through the gap in the neckline, and then stuff firmly with toy filling. Ladder stitch the opening closed (see Stitching Techniques), stuffing in a little more as you go to avoid a dimple.

17 Using the pink pencil, draw and colour in the cheek circles on Molly's face. Take your narrow ribbon and cut in half; use each length to tie a bow around the base of Molly's bunches.

TIP
For a more permanent fixing, secure the bow knots with a spot of fabric glue.

Rufus the Robot

Finished size: 25cm (10in) tall

Rufus the Robot is ready for action at the flick of a switch – he is programmed to be a child's best friend, to help with chores like cleaning up a messy bedroom or cooking up a midnight snack. And if only that were so, who wouldn't want a Rufus of their own! When switched off, he will spend his time sitting on a bedroom shelf, legs dangling, patiently awaiting activation.

Construction of this robot is fairly quick and he can be made up with any of your child's favourite prints. He is perfect for beginners who want to stretch themselves to the next level.

YOU WILL NEED

Note: Buttons should be omitted if making this toy for a very small child.

* 12.5 x 81cm (5 x 32in) cream patterned fabric (head)
* 12.5 x 63.5cm (5 x 25in) blue space print fabric (body)
* 15 x 66cm (6in x 26in) red star print fabric (headlights, hands, feet)
* 36cm (14in) lightweight fusible fleece
* 25cm (10in) of 2cm (¾in) wide twill tape (arms, legs)
* Six-strand embroidery thread (floss): black
* Two medium black buttons for eyes
* Two medium red buttons for buttons
* Good quality polyester thread
* Good quality toy filling

Cutting Your Fabrics

Note: Trace the Robot templates (see Templates) onto tracing paper or template plastic, transferring all of the markings, and cut them out along the traced lines.

From your cream patterned fabric

First interface the fabric piece with fusible fleece, then cut the following pieces from the interfaced fabric.

Cut two pieces measuring 11 x 15cm (4¼ x 6in).

Cut two pieces measuring 7.5 x 15cm (3 x 6in).

Cut two pieces measuring 11 x 7.5cm (4¼ x 3in).

From your blue space print fabric

First interface the fabric piece with fusible fleece, then cut the following pieces from the interfaced fabric.

Cut two pieces measuring 11 x 11.5cm (4¼ x 4½in).

Cut two pieces measuring 7.5 x 11.5cm (3 x 4½in).

Cut two pieces measuring 11 x 7.5cm (4¼ x 3in).

From your red star print fabric

Trace the headlights template twice onto the fabric and cut out along the traced line.

Cut one piece measuring 7.5 x 15cm (3 x 6in) for the hands.

Now interface the remaining fabric with the fusible fleece, then cut the following pieces from the interfaced fabric.

Cut one piece measuring 7.5 x 15cm (3 x 6in) for the hands.

Cut twelve squares measuring 4.5 x 4.5cm (1¾ x 1¾in) for the feet.

Preparing to Start

1 Take the fleece-backed red star print fabric measuring 7.5 x 15cm (3 x 6in) and trace the hand template twice onto the wrong (fleece-backed) side, allowing at least 1cm (⅜in) between each tracing.

2 Cut the twill tape into four lengths each measuring 5–5.5cm (2–2¼in).

3 Set your sewing machine to a small stitch length of approx 1.5 for stitching the toy and use a good quality polyester thread for strong seams.

Making the Robot

Note: A 6mm (¼in) seam allowance is included in all pattern pieces unless advised otherwise. Read through all instructions before beginning to avoid surprises.

1 To make the robot's face, take one of the cream patterned fabric pieces measuring 11 x 15cm (4¼ x 6in) and working about 3.25cm (1¼in) up from the bottom edge, mark the mouth (see template) centring it on the fabric width. Using all six strands of black embroidery thread (floss), backstitch along the marked line. Sew on a black button eye to either side of the mouth (see Fig. 1).

Fig. 1

3 Sew together the short ends of this panel to create a ring, starting and ending your stitching 6mm (¼in) from each corner. This is the head gusset ring.

4 Taking your head gusset ring and the face piece, match up one of the longer edges of the head gusset ring with the top edge of the face, right sides together. Sew together, starting and ending 6mm (¼in) from the corners (these start and end points should correlate with the stitching start points on the gusset seams to create a corner). Now match up the other long edge of the head gusset ring with the bottom edge of the face, again right sides together, and sew together as before. Now continue to sew the shorter edges of the head gusset ring to the side edges of the face in the same way.

5 Now join the final 11 x 15cm (4¼ x 6in) piece of the cream patterned fabric to the head gusset ring to complete the back of the robot's head. Join the back of the head to the head gusset ring as described in step 4, always starting and ending your stitching 6mm (¼in) from the corners. **Do not** leave a turning gap.

2 Take one cream patterned fabric piece measuring 11 x 7.5cm (4¼ x 3in) and another piece measuring 7.5 x 15cm (3 x 6in), place one on top of the other with right sides together aligning along the short edges. Sew together starting and ending your stitches 6mm (¼in) from each corner (see Fig. 2a), and continue in the same way to join another 11 x 7.5cm (4¼ x 3in) piece and the final 7.5 x 15cm (3 x 6in) piece to create a panel as in Fig. 2b.

Fig. 2a

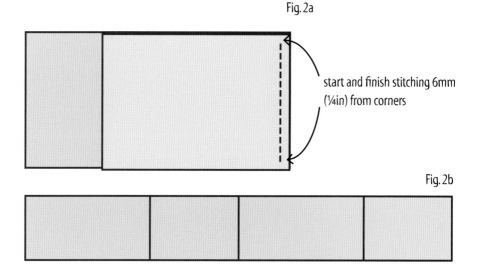

start and finish stitching 6mm (¼in) from corners

Fig. 2b

7 To make one of the robot's legs, take six of the red star print squares and one of your lengths of twill tape. Place two squares on top of each other with right sides together and lay the twill tape in between so that the raw edge of the tape is centred and aligned with one of the edges of the fabric squares as shown in Fig. 3. Sew the layers together along this edge, starting and ending your stitching 6mm (¼in) from the corners (see Fig. 3).

Fig. 3

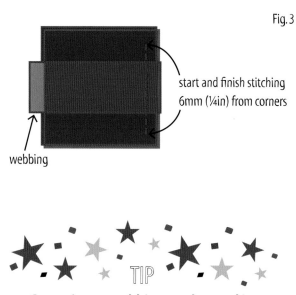

start and finish stitching
6mm (¼in) from corners

webbing

6 To turn the completed head through to the right side, you need to make a slit in the centre of the base gusset panel approx 5cm (2in) long. This slit will be hidden against the robot's body when the head is sewn in place. Turn the head through the slit and stuff it with toy filling. Whip stitch the gap closed (remember this will be hidden so there is no need to be super neat). Put the head aside for now.

TIP

Strapping or webbing can be used in place of twill tape, just as long as its tough enough to endure play!

TIP

One of the easiest way to create a slit with added control is to use a seam ripper (quick unpick).

8 Join two more red star print squares to make a panel of four joined squares, then join the short ends into a ring (as you did for the head gusset ring). Always remember to start and end your stitching 6mm (¼in) from each corner and take care not to catch the twill tape as you sew.

9 Take the remaining two red star-print squares and sew these in to each side of the ring to create a cube in the same way as you did when making the head, but this time when sewing one of the edges, leave a 2cm (¾in) turning gap in the centre of the stitching line. Turn the foot right side out.

10 Repeat steps 7–9 to make a second leg for your robot. (Note: the feet will be stuffed later in the making process.)

11 To make the robot's arms, start by taking the two pieces of red star-print fabric measuring 7.5 x 15cm (3 x 6in) and place them on top of each other with right sides together. Working fleece-side up, sew along the traced lines of the hands, leaving the straight ends unstitched as indicated by the broken line on the template. Cut out each hand approx 3mm (⅛in) outside your sewn lines, and then turn the hands right side out. Fold the raw edges in by approx 6mm (¼in) and press folds in place.

12 Lightly stuff the hands with toy filling. Take the remaining twill tape pieces and insert one end of each into the open ends of the hand, pushing them in by approx 6mm (¼in). Topstitch along the folded in edges to catch the twill tape lengths in place to complete the arms.

13 Take one of your blue space print fabric pieces measuring 11 x 11.5cm (4¼ x 4½in) and sew on two red buttons in the centre approx 1.5cm (⅝in) down from the top edge (see Fig. 4). This is the front of the robot's body.

Fig. 4

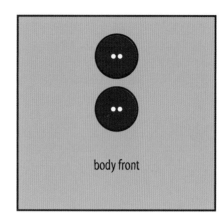

body front

14 Now place your arms and legs in position onto the body front as in Fig. 5, so that the arms are approx 2cm (¾in) down from the top corners and placed at an angle and the legs are approx 2.5cm (1in) apart from the centre of the bottom edge. Machine tack (baste) the limbs in place close to the edge.

Fig. 5

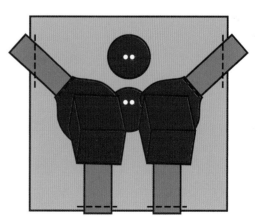

15 Take the blue space-print fabric pieces measuring 7.5 x 11.5cm (3 x 4½in) and 11 x 7.5cm (4¼ x 3in) and sew together alternately along the 7.5cm (3in) edges to create a panel, then join the short ends of the panel to make the body gusset ring, in the same way as you did to make the head gusset ring (see steps 2 and 3), starting and ending your stitches 6mm (¼in) from each corner.

16 Take your body gusset ring and the body front and match up one of the longer edges of the body gusset ring to the top edge of the body front, right sides together. Sew together, starting and ending 6mm (¼in) from the corners (these start and end points should correlate with the stitching start points on the gusset seams to create a corner).

17 Now match up the other long edge of the body gusset ring with the bottom edge of the body front, again right sides together, and sew together as before. Now continue to sew the shorter edges of the body gusset ring to the sides of the body front in the same way, making sure to catch the arms in the seams as you sew.

18 Now join the final 11 x 11.5cm (4¼ x 4½in) piece of the blue space print fabric to the body gusset ring to complete the back of the robot's body in the same way, always stopping and starting 6mm (¼in) from the corners. **Do not** leave a turning gap.

19 To turn the completed body through to the right side, you need to make a slit in the centre of the top gusset approx 6.5cm (2½in) long. This slit will be hidden against the robot's head when the body and head are sewn together. Turn the body through the slit and stuff it with toy filling. Whip stitch the gap closed (remember this will be hidden so there is no need to be super neat). To complete the stuffing, fill the feet firmly with toy filling, and ladder stitch the turning gap closed (see Stitching Techniques).

20 To join the body and the head, place the head so it sits neatly centred on the body. Using two strands of strong polyester thread, ladder stitch the body to the head (see Stitching Techniques) stitching together just outside the seam along all edges to give a neat join. Go around your stitching twice, pulling tightly as you go to form a firm strong attachment.

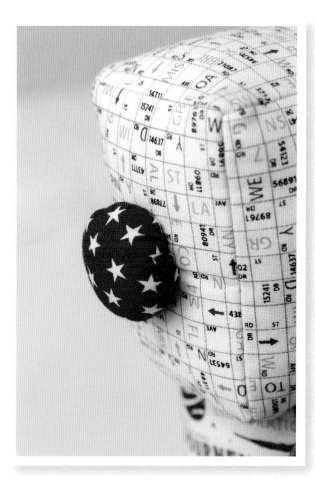

21 To make the first headlight, take one of your red star print fabric circles and, securing the end of your thread with a knot, make small hand running stitches all the way around the raw edge. When you reach your start point, pull the thread to gather the circle, and when it is half gathered, place a little stuffing into the centre, then gather it up all the way, securing the gathers with a knot. Make a second headlight with the remaining star print circle.

22 Ladder stitch a headlight to each side of the robot's head (refer to the close up photo as a positioning guide). (see Stitching Techniques: Attaching Parts). Work the ladder stitch in a circle and go around at least twice to ensure the headlights are firmly attached.

Yumi the Unicorn

Finished size: 28cm (11in) tall

As the sun shines through the rain clouds and a rainbow arches across the sky, if you are very lucky, and if you take the time to look very closely, you may just catch a glimpse of Yumi the Unicorn. She loves to frolic at the end of the rainbow – it's her favourite place to play, although with all her bright colours she can be very difficult to spot there.

Construction of Yumi requires a little more patience and accuracy for the placing of the inner legs during construction and the addition of ric-rac between the seams. Choose fun, bright, playful fabrics for a true fantasyland feel and lots of different colours of ric-rac to create an eye-catching rainbow mane.

YOU WILL NEED

Note: Buttons should be omitted if making this toy for a very small child.

* 25 x 86.5cm (10 x 34in) main patterned fabric (body, inner legs)
* 12.5 x 86.5cm (5 x 34in) coordinating patterned fabric (hooves, ears)
* 10 x 7.5cm (4 x 3in) stripe fabric (horn)
* 5 x 7.5cm (2 x 3in) lightweight fusible fleece
* 2m (2¼yd) each of four coordinating colours of mini ric-rac (mane/tail)
* Two small black buttons for eyes
* Good quality polyester thread
* Good quality toy filling

Cutting Your Fabrics

Note: Trace the Unicorn templates (see Templates) onto tracing paper or template plastic, transferring all of the markings, and cut them out along the traced lines. When using these templates to trace the pattern pieces onto your fabric, do ensure that the marked grain line on the template matches the grain line of your fabric.

From your coordinating patterned fabric

Cut one strip measuring 5 x 86.5cm (2 x 34in).

Cut one piece measuring 7.5 x 10cm (3 x 4in).

Fold the remaining fabric in half with right sides together. Trace the hoof base template twice onto the folded fabric and cut out along the traced line to give you four hoof pieces.

Preparing to Start

1 Interface one half of the 7.5 x 10cm (3 x 4in) piece of your coordinating patterned fabric with your piece of lightweight fusible fleece.

2 Set your sewing machine to a small stitch length of approx 1.5 for stitching the toy and use a good-quality polyester thread for strong seams.

Making the Unicorn

Note: A 6mm (¼in) seam allowance is included in all pattern pieces unless advised otherwise. Read through all instructions before beginning to avoid surprises.

1 Take your main patterned fabric piece measuring 25 x 86.5cm (10 x 34in) and your strip of coordinating patterned fabric measuring 5 x 86.5cm (2 x 34in); place the fabric pieces on top of each other with right sides together, and then stitch to join along one long edge to make the body/hoof fabric panel. Press the seam open. Fold your fabric panel in half width ways with right sides together so that the short edges meet and fabrics and seams meet evenly.

2 Place the body template and the inner leg template onto the folded fabric panel, making sure to line up the bottom (straight) edge of both templates with the raw edge of the coordinating patterned (narrower) fabric strip, which will become the unicorn's hooves. Trace around each template once and then cut out along the traced lines to give you two body pieces and two inner leg pieces.

3 Take one body piece and the matching inner leg piece and place them on top of each other with right sides together. Referring to Fig. 1, sew the inner leg to the body ensuring that you start sewing right at the raw edge of the fabric at the top of the inner leg piece and then gradually turn into a 6mm (¼in) seam. **Do not** sew the bottom straight edges of the hooves together. Very carefully snip the inner leg curves. **Do not** turn through to the right side. Repeat to join the remaining body and inner leg pieces.

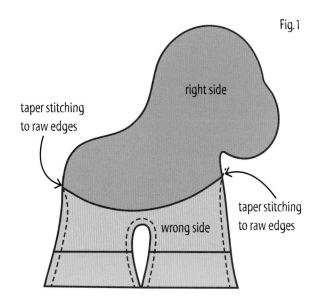

Fig.1

taper stitching to raw edges

right side

taper stitching to raw edges

wrong side

4 Sew the darts in place on the wrong side of each of the inner leg pieces as indicated on the template.

5 Take one of the hoof base pieces and ease this into place along the bottom raw edge of one of the legs, right sides together. It is essential to tack (baste) or pin well, and, when you are happy with the fit, sew the hoof base into place at the end of the leg. To ensure there is no puckering, it will help after each small section is sewn if you stop stitching, with the needle down, and rotate and smooth the leg fabric underneath before continuing. Complete all four legs.

6 Take your four lengths of mini ric-rac and place together evenly to form a bundle. Cut the bundle into eight 23cm (9in) lengths to form eight individual bundles, one for the tail and seven for the mane.

7 To make the unicorn's tail, take one of your ric-rac bundles and fold it in half. Place the bundle onto the tail end of one of your joined body/inner leg pieces so that the folded end rests just outside the raw edge of the fabric (see body template for position). Machine tack (baste) the tail in position (see Fig. 2).

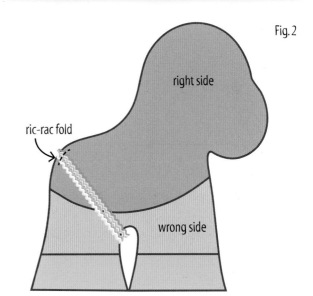

Fig. 2

right side

ric-rac fold

wrong side

8 To make the unicorn's mane, fold your remaining seven ric-rac bundles in half and place them evenly along the unicorn's head (see body template for position) so that the folded ends rest just outside the raw edge of the fabric. Machine tack (baste) the mane in position (see Fig. 3).

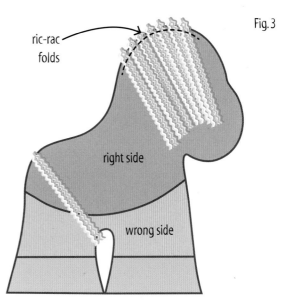

Fig. 3

ric-rac folds

right side

wrong side

9 Place one body piece on top of the other with right sides together, with the inner legs in between. Tack (baste) together starting from one end of the turning gap to the other as marked on the body template. When you reach the inner leg section, ensure that you are tacking (basting) the top straight edges of the inner legs together, right sides facing. You may find it easier to do this by folding the legs up against either side of the body (see Fig. 4).

Fig. 4

wrong side

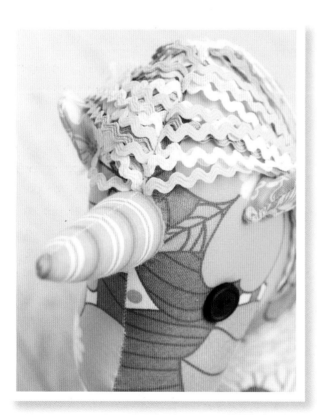

TIP

When tacking (basting), make sure that the mane and tail are well clear of the edges so that they do not get caught in your stitching.

10 Sew the body together leaving the turning gap open. Carefully snip any curved and angled edges along the seam before turning the unicorn right side out.

11 Stuff the unicorn very firmly with toy filling making sure that the legs in particular are well stuffed to ensure the unicorn can stand up. Using strong polyester thread, ladder stitch the opening closed (see Stitching Techniques), stuffing in a little more as you go to avoid a dimple.

12 Trim the unicorn's mane and tail to neaten and shape as desired.

★ ★ ★ ★ ★ ★ ★
TIP
To keep the ric-rac neat, paint a little fray stopper or fabric glue on the end of each length.

13 Now to make the ears. Take your small piece of fleece-backed coordinating patterned fabric and fold in half, right sides together, so that one side is interfaced and the other is not. Trace the ear template twice onto the interfaced side, and then sew along the traced lines leaving the turning gaps open as indicated by the broken line on the template. Cut out each ear approx 3mm (⅛in) outside your sewn line; snip corners, turn through to the right side and press.

14 Using strong polyester thread, ladder stitch an ear onto either side of the unicorn's head (see Stitching Techniques). I chose to ladder stitch the ears in place in a folded shape.

15 To make the horn, take your piece of stripe fabric and fold in half with right sides together. Trace the horn template once onto the folded fabric, and then sew along the traced line, leaving the end unstitched as indicated by the broken line on the template. Cut out the horn approx 3mm (⅛in) outside the sewn line and turn right side out. Fold the raw ends of the turning gap in by approx 6mm (¼in) and finger press in place. Stuff the horn firmly with toy filling.

16 Position the horn where desired on your unicorn's head or refer to the photographs as a guide to positioning. Hold the horn in place by pinning through the horn and into the head, much like a pin cushion. Using strong polyester thread, ladder stitch the horn in place on the head working the ladder stitch in a circle (see Stitching Techniques: Attaching Parts). When you get approx three quarters of the way around, stuff the horn a little bit more to make sure it is nice and firm. I recommend you stitch around at least twice to ensure the horn is firmly attached.

17 Using black thread, sew the button eyes into place on the unicorn's face. Pull the thread to indent the eyes ever so slightly if desired.

Fifi the Fairy

Finished size: 33cm (13in) tall

F lying daintily from rose bush to rose bush, you simply cannot miss Fifi the Fairy. She has fabulous pink floral hair swept up into buns that sit neatly atop her head, and with her delicate rosebud print top and her sweetly gathered polka dot miniskirt, she is a fashion trendsetter in the fairy world. With her cheeky grin, she is sure to capture a little girl's heart when she flies into her bedroom.

Construction of Fifi involves preparing lots of different small elements that are all eventually sewn together, and as everything is sewn so securely without any buttons or small attachments, she is perfect for even the littlest of hands.

YOU WILL NEED

- ★ 35.5 x 35.5cm (14 x 14in) pink floral print fabric (hair, head back, bottom wings)
- ★ 20 x 30.5cm (8 x 12in) aqua patterned fabric (body)
- ★ 18 x 56cm (7 x 22in) pink spot print fabric (skirt, top wings)
- ★ 18 x 61cm (7 x 24in) plain fabric (face, arms, legs)
- ★ 15 x 20cm (6 x 8in) lightweight fusible fleece
- ★ 12.5 x 20cm (5 x 8in) fusible web
- ★ Six-strand embroidery thread (floss): dark grey, pink
- ★ Pink pencil
- ★ Good quality polyester thread
- ★ Good quality toy filling

Cutting Your Fabrics

Note: Trace the Fairy templates (see Templates) onto tracing paper or template plastic, transferring all of the markings, and cut them out along the traced lines. When using these templates to trace the pattern pieces onto your fabric, do ensure that the marked grain line on the template matches the grain line of your fabric.

From your pink floral print fabric

Cut one piece measuring 18 x 18cm (7 x 7in) for hair.

Cut one piece measuring 7.5 x 30.5cm (3 x 12in) for bottom wings.

Trace the head template once for the head back and the hair bun template twice onto the remaining fabric and cut out along the traced lines.

From your aqua patterned fabric

Fold fabric in half with right sides together. Trace the body top and body bottom templates once each onto folded fabric and cut out along the traced lines to give you two body tops and two body bottoms.

Unfold remaining fabric and trace the body base template once; cut out along the traced line.

From your pink spot-print

Cut one strip measuring 9 x 56cm (3½ x 22in) for the skirt.

Cut one piece measuring 7.5 x 35.5cm (3 x 14in) for the top wings.

From your plain fabric

Cut one piece measuring 18 x 18cm (7 x 7in) for the face.

Fold the remaining fabric in half with right sides together. Trace the arm and leg templates twice each onto the folded fabric, but **do not** cut out (these will be sewn on the traced line).

Preparing to Start

1 Interface one half only of each of your wing fabric pieces with lightweight fusible fleece.

2 Trace the hairline template onto the paper side of the fusible web and rough cut out close to the traced line. Fuse this hairline piece to the wrong side of your piece of pink floral-print fabric for the hair measuring 18 x 18cm (7 x 7in), positioning it centrally along the bottom edge.

3 Set your sewing machine to a small stitch length of approx 1.5 for stitching the toy and use a good quality polyester thread for strong seams.

Making the Fairy

Note: A 6mm (¼in) seam allowance is included in all pattern pieces unless advised otherwise. Read through all instructions before beginning to avoid surprises.

1 Take your pink floral print fabric for the hair (with fusible web attached) and cut along the traced line from the bottom edge of the hairline only, so that you have a piece remaining as shown in Fig. 1.

Fig. 1

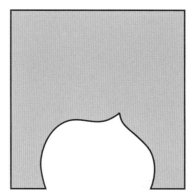

2 Peel the backing paper away from the fusible web on this hair piece, then position it onto your piece of plain fabric for the face, making sure there is adequate plain fabric below the hairline to be able to fit in the doll's face template. Fuse in place. Machine appliqué the bottom hairline edge onto the plain fabric: I used machine buttonhole stitch.

3 Take the head template and trace this onto the hair/face fabric panel created in step 2, so that the appliquéd hairline meets the hairline on the template. Cut the head out along the traced line. Cut away any excess plain fabric (above fused section) from the wrong side of the front head. Put aside for now.

4 Take your folded piece of plain fabric with the arms and legs traced onto it and, keeping the fabric folded, sew along the traced lines of the arms and legs, leaving the straight ends unstitched as indicated by the broken line on the templates. Cut out limbs approx 3–6mm (⅛– ¼in) outside your sewn lines, and then turn right side out.

5 Firmly stuff the limbs to the very ends with toy filling, leaving the last 2cm (¾in) unstuffed. Tack (baste) the open ends closed.

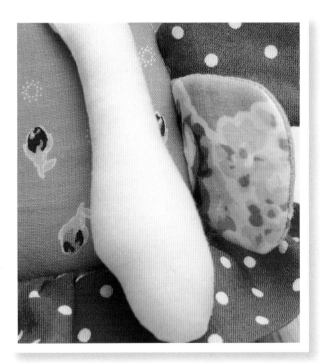

6 Take one of the body top pieces and place it right side up on your work surface. Place the arms on top of the body top piece aligning the raw edge of the arms with the raw edge of the neckline and positioning the arms approx 3–6mm (⅛– ¼in) in from the sides; machine tack (baste) in position close to the raw edge (see Fig. 2).

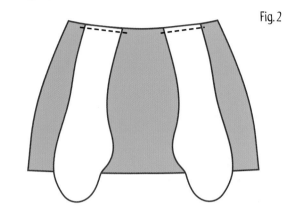

Fig. 2

7 Take your set aside front head and front body top with arms and place on top of each other with right sides together so that they are aligned at the neckline. Pin in place, and then sew along the neckline. This is the joined front piece.

8 Take your remaining body top and head back pieces and place on top of each other with right sides together, so that they are aligned at the neckline. Pin in place, and then sew along the neckline, leaving the middle section open for turning and stuffing as indicated by the broken line on the body top template. This is the joined back piece.

TIP

Crisp edges on your turning gap makes stitching it closed in step 20 a little easier, so press the seam and turning gap allowance open after joining the body and head back pieces together.

9 Take your pink spot print wing piece and fold it in half, right sides together, so that one side is interfaced and the other is not. Trace the top wing template twice onto the interfaced side, flipping the template for your second tracing. Then sew along the traced lines leaving the turning gaps open as indicated by the broken line on the template.

10 Repeat step 9 with your pink floral print wing fabric piece and your bottom wing template. Cut all of the wings out approx 3mm (⅛in) outside the sewn lines, turn right side out and press.

11 Place the joined front piece right side up on your work surface and then position the wings on top of this, right sides together, so that the straight edges of the wings meet the raw edges of the body top: first place the bottom wings, then the top wings so that they overlap by approx 1cm (⅜in) and machine tack (baste) into place (see Fig. 3).

Fig. 3

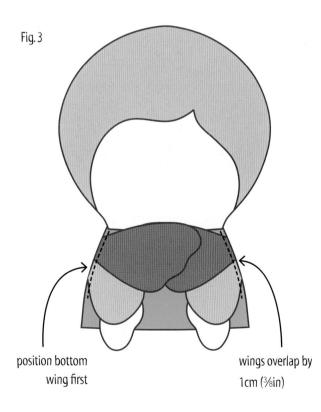

position bottom wing first

wings overlap by 1cm (⅜in)

12 Take the fairy front with wings and the fairy back piece and place on top of each other, right sides together. Sew together along the sides of the body top and around the head (you will be securing the wings in place as you stitch) leaving the bottom edge of the body top open. **Do not** turn the body top right side out. To make the forthcoming steps a little easier, fold the arms up to sit inside the head section at this stage.

TIP

When sewing body front and back together make sure the arms and wings are well clear to avoid catching them in your stitching.

13 Take your strip of pink spot print skirt fabric and fold in half lengthways with wrong sides together, so that the strip measures 4.5 x 56cm (1¾ x 22in). Press well. Unfold the strip, join the short ends with right sides together to create a ring, and sew. Refold the fabric along the previous fold line, wrong sides together, and press once again.

14 Take a long length of doubled polyester thread and securing the start point with a knot, take small to medium hand running stitches all the way around the raw edge of your folded fabric ring, and when you reach your start point, pull up your thread to gather the top edge to begin to gather the skirt. Gather the top edge of the skirt evenly until it measures the same circumference as the bottom edge of the body top, then tie off your thread end securely so that the skirt ruffles cannot loosen.

15 Take the inside-out body top and place the gathered skirt inside the open bottom edge, so that the raw edge of the gathered skirt aligns with the raw edge of the body opening, right sides together. Machine tack (baste) in place all the way around the body opening approx 3mm (⅛in) from the raw edges.

16 Take the two aqua patterned body bottom pieces, place on top of each other with right sides together, and sew along the short side edges only. Now take the body base piece and ease this evenly into position along the bottom raw edge of the body bottom (still inside out) with right sides together. (You may find this is easier to do by marking the quarter points on your base and body bottom and then matching these up.) It is essential to tack (baste) or pin well first.

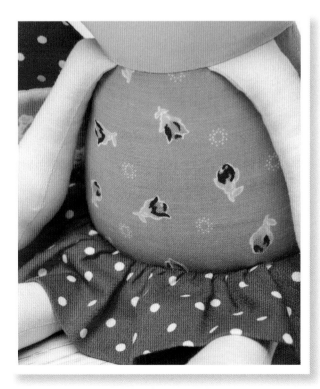

17 When you are happy with the fit, sew the body base into place, leaving the leg gaps open as indicated by the broken lines on your body bottom template. To ensure there is no puckering, it will help after each small section is sewn if you stop stitching, with the needle down, and rotate and smooth the fabric underneath before continuing. Turn the joined bottom body/base right side out.

18 Take your still inside-out body top and fit the body bottom inside the opening over the gathered skirt, right sides together. Make sure that the leg opening side of the body bottom is facing the body front and that all the raw edges are evenly aligned. You should now have the bottom raw edge of the body top, the raw edge of the gathered skirt and the top raw edge of the body bottom meeting evenly together. Pin or tack (baste) well and then sew the three layers into place. **Do not** turn through to the right side.

19 Still working on the inside-out body, insert one of the legs, raw edges first, through the turning gap on the back of the neckline. Guide the raw edges into one of the leg gaps on the body bottom, making sure that the raw edge of the leg aligns with the raw edge of the leg gap and that the toe is facing outwards. Following the stitching line on the body base, sew the leg in place. Repeat to sew the second leg in the remaining leg gap.

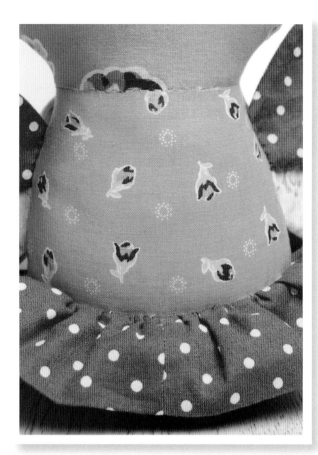

20 Carefully and methodically turn the completed fairy right sides out through the gap in the neckline, and then stuff firmly with toy filling. Ladder stitch the opening closed (see Stitching Techniques) stuffing a little more as you go to avoid a dimple.

TIP
When turning limb-laden toys, always start by turning though the stuffed limbs, beginning with those closest to the turning. Once the limbs are neatly through the rest of the fabric will follow naturally.

21 Take one of your pink floral-print bun circles and securing the end of your thread with a knot, make small hand running stitches all the way around the raw edge (see Stitching Techniques). When you reach your start point, pull the thread to gather the circle. When it is half gathered, place a little stuffing into the centre, then gather it up all the way, securing the gathers with a knot. Referring to Stitching Techniques: Attaching Parts, ladder stitch the bun in a circle to the side of the fairy's head (see photograph for positioning). I recommend you sew around the circle twice for added strength. Repeat for the second bun.

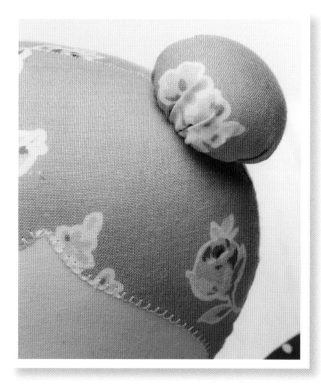

22 Mark the eyes and mouth onto Fifi's face. Sinking your knots before you start (see Stitching Techniques), create the eyes with satin stitch using two strands of dark grey embroidery thread (floss), then continue with the same thread to backstitch the eyelashes. Using two strands of pink embroidery thread (floss), backstitch the mouth. Using the pink pencil, draw and colour in the cheek circles.

Super Scotty

Finished size: 33cm (13in) tall

Is it a bird? Is it a plane? No, it's Super Scotty! Able to leap tall bunk beds in a single bound, this boy of steel is ready to fight the battle for toy box justice. Take off his cape and his mask and you may mistake him for any ordinary boy, but in one quick change he becomes a superhero who will be sure to keep any child's bedroom full of adventure and action.

Construction of Super Scotty is not so tricky but as it involves a number of different steps and techniques, he gets an advanced rating. With patience, however, he is certainly very achievable for intermediate sewers, too.

YOU WILL NEED

- ★ 18 x 35.5cm (7 x 14in) brown dot print fabric (head back, hair)
- ★ 30.5 x 38cm (12 x 15in) green patterned fabric (body, legs, arms)
- ★ 38 x 38cm (15 x 15in) red spot print fabric (boots, pants, cape)
- ★ 25 x 25cm (10 x 10in) plain skin-coloured fabric (head front, hands)
- ★ 15 x 15cm (6 x 6in) red wool felt (mask, star)
- ★ 5 x 5cm (2 x 2in) white wool felt (chest circle)
- ★ 25cm (10in) of 5mm (¼in) wide elastic for mask
- ★ 30cm (12in) of 1.3cm (½in) wide red ribbon for cape ties
- ★ 18 x 28cm (7 x 11in) fusible web
- ★ Six-strand embroidery thread (floss): brown, red
- ★ Good quality polyester thread
- ★ Good quality toy filling

Cutting Your Fabrics

Note: Trace the Super Scotty templates (see Templates) onto tracing paper or template plastic, transferring all the markings, and cut them out along the traced lines. When using these templates to trace the pattern pieces onto your fabric, do ensure that the marked grain line on the template matches the grain line of your fabric.

From your brown dot print fabric

Cut one piece measuring 18 x 18cm (7 x 7in) for hair.

Fold the remaining fabric in half, right sides together. Trace head template once onto the folded fabric and cut out along traced line to give you one head back.

From your green patterned fabric

Cut two strips measuring 7.5 x 25cm (3 x 10in) for the arms and legs.

Cut two pieces measuring 7.5 x 5cm (3 x 2in) for the body base.

Fold remaining fabric in half with right sides together. Trace the body template once onto the folded fabric and cut out along the traced lines to give you two body pieces.

From your red spot print fabric

Cut one strip measuring 10 x 25cm (4 x 10in) for boots.

Cut one piece measuring 12.5 x 15cm (5 x 6in) for the pants (front and back).

Cut one piece measuring 7.5 x 5cm (3 x 2in) for the pants gusset.

Fold remaining fabric in half with right sides together. Trace the cape template twice onto the folded fabric, but **do not** cut out (this will be sewn on the traced line).

From your plain (skin-coloured) fabric

Cut one piece measuring 18 x 18cm (7 x 7in) for face.

Cut one piece measuring 6.5 x 25cm (2½ x 10in) for the hands.

Preparing to Start

1   Trace the hairline template onto the paper side of the fusible web; rough cut out close to the traced line. Fuse this hairline piece to the wrong side of your brown dot print fabric measuring 18 x 18cm (7 x 7in), positioning it centrally along the bottom edge.

2   Trace the chest circle and star templates onto the paper side of the fusible web and rough cut out. Fuse the chest circle to the white felt and the star to the red felt, and then cut out along the traced lines.

3   Trace the pants shape from the body template twice onto the paper side of the fusible web, rough cut out, and then fuse to the red spot print fabric piece measuring 12.5 x 15cm (5 x 6in). Cut out along the traced lines.

4   Set your sewing machine to a small stitch length of approx 1.5 for stitching the toy and use a good quality polyester thread for strong seams.

Making Super Scotty

Note: A 6mm (¼in) seam allowance is included in all pattern pieces unless advised otherwise. Read through all instructions before beginning to avoid surprises.

1 Take your brown dot-print fabric for the hair (with fusible web attached) and cut along the traced line from the bottom edge of the hairline only, so that you have a piece remaining as shown in Fig. 1.

Fig. 1

2 Peel the backing paper away from the remaining fusible web on the wrong side of the brown dot-print fabric, then position and fuse the hair piece onto your piece of plain (skin-coloured) fabric for the face, making sure to position it so that there is adequate plain fabric below the hairline to be able to fit in Scotty's face template. Machine appliqué the bottom hairline edge onto the plain fabric: I used two lines of raw edge appliqué.

3 Take your head template and trace this onto the hair/face fabric panel created in step 2, so that the appliquéd hairline meets the hairline on the template and cut out along the traced line. Cut away any excess plain fabric (above fused section) from the wrong side of the front head piece. Put aside for now.

4 Take one of the green patterned fabric strips and one of the plain (skin-coloured) fabric strips each measuring 25cm (10in) long and place them on top of each other, right sides together. Sew together along one 25cm (10in) edge, open out the joined panel and press. Fold the panel in half width ways, so that the short edges meet and right sides are together, making sure that the fabrics and seam line are perfectly aligned. Place the arm template onto the folded fabric panel making sure that the marked hand line matches up with the seam in the fabric. Trace around the template twice, flipping the template for the second trace. **Do not** cut out (see Fig. 2).

Fig. 2

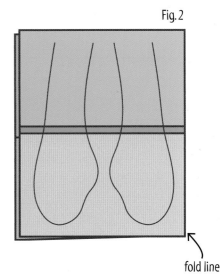

fold line

5 Referring to step 4, make a fabric panel for the legs from your remaining green patterned fabric strip and the red spot print strip, each measuring 25cm (10in) long. Fold the panel in half width ways, so that the short edges meet and right sides are together, making sure that the fabrics and seam line are perfectly aligned. Place the leg template onto the folded fabric panel so that the marked boot line matches up with the seam in the fabric and draw around the template twice, flipping the template for the second trace. **Do not** cut out.

6 Keeping each of the fabric panels folded, sew along the traced lines of the arms and the legs, leaving the straight ends unstitched as indicated by the broken line on the templates. Cut out each limb approx 3–6mm (⅛– ¼in) outside your sewn lines and then turn the limbs right side out. Firmly stuff the limbs to the very ends with toy filling, leaving the last 2cm (¾in) unstuffed. Tack (baste) the open ends closed.

7 Take your front body and back body green patterned fabric pieces and fuse a red spot-print pants shape to the bottom edge of each, and machine appliqué in place. Take the front body piece and fuse and machine appliqué the white felt circle to the chest, positioning it approx 6mm (¼in) above the top edge of the pants. Fuse and machine appliqué the red felt star in the centre of the white circle.

8 Place the front body piece right side up on your work surface. Place the arms on top aligning the raw edge of the arms with the raw edge of the neckline and positioning the arms approx 1.3cm (½in) in from the sides. Machine tack (baste) in position close to the raw edge (see Fig. 3).

Fig. 3

9 Take the front head and the front body with arms pieces that you set aside and place these on top of each other with right sides together so that they are aligned at the neckline. Pin in place, and then sew together along the neckline.

10 Take the remaining back body and back head pieces and place on top of each other with right sides together so that they are aligned at the neckline. Pin in place, and then sew along the neckline, leaving the middle section open for turning and stuffing as indicated by the broken line on the body template.

11 Take your front body/head and your back body/head and place on top of each other, right sides together. Sew together along the sides of the body and around the head, leaving the bottom edge of the body open. **Do not** turn right side out; to make forthcoming steps a little easier, fold the arms up to sit inside the head section at this stage.

12 Now take one of the legs and insert it foot first, with toe facing inwards, into the opening at the bottom edge of the body. Centre the leg within one of the side green sections of the front body and align the raw edge of the leg with the raw edge of the bottom edge of the front body. Machine tack (baste) in place to the front body only. Repeat to position the second leg on the other side green section of the front body (see Fig. 4).

Fig. 4

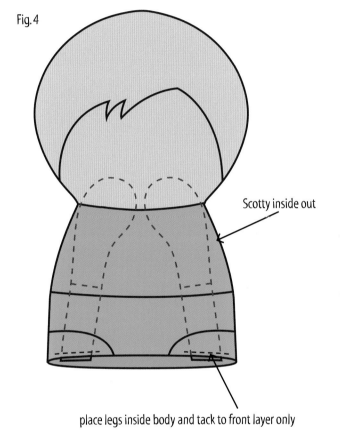

Scotty inside out

place legs inside body and tack to front layer only

13 Take the 7.5 x 5cm (3 x 2in) red spot fabric piece and the two remaining green patterned fabric pieces the same size and sew these together along the 7.5cm (3in) edges to create a panel (see Fig. 5). Press the seams open. This is the fabric panel for cutting out the body base template. Working on the wrong side of your fabric, trace the body base template onto the fabric panel so that the marked pants lines match up with the seams, and then cut the base out along the traced line.

Fig. 5

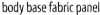

body base fabric panel

14 Take the body base piece and ease this evenly into position along the bottom raw edge of the body (still inside out) with right sides together. You may find this is easier to do by first matching up the pants seams at the body front and back, then continue easing the body base into position around the remaining edges. It is essential to tack (baste) or pin well first, and then, when you are happy with the fit, sew the body base into place. To ensure there is no puckering, it will help after each small section is sewn if you stop stitching, with the needle down, to rotate and smooth the fabric underneath before continuing.

15 Turn the body right sides out through the neckline gap and stuff firmly with toy filling. Ladder stitch the opening closed (see Stitching Techniques) stuffing in a little more toy filling as you go to avoid a dimple.

16 Mark the eyes and mouth onto Scotty's face. Sinking your knots before you start (see Stitching Techniques), create the eyes with satin stitch using two strands of brown embroidery thread (floss), and backstitch the mouth using two strands of red embroidery thread (floss).

17 Take the red spot print fabric with the cape traced onto it and, keeping the fabric folded, sew along the traced line, leaving the top edge open as indicated by the broken line on the cape template. Cut out approx 3mm (⅛in) outside the sewn line, snipping the corners. Turn right side out and press. Leaving the top edge open, topstitch along the three sewn edges.

18 Take your ribbon trim and fold it in half lengthways with wrong sides together. Press well. Now take the cape and place the open edge inside the folded trim, so that it is centred along the length of the ribbon. Tack (baste) in place. Topstitch along the full length of the trim catching the cape securely in your stitching (see Fig. 6). Fit the cape around Scotty's neck and tie at the front.

topstitch ribbon trim　　　　Fig. 6

19 To make Scotty's mask, trace the mask template twice onto the remaining red felt. Using small sharp scissors, cut out neatly. Pin or tack (baste) the two mask pieces together and topstitch along the outside edge, leaving two gaps at the sides as indicated by the broken line on the template. Topstitch also around the eye holes, then trim any uneven edges to neaten. Take your elastic and insert one end into one of the gaps at the side of the mask; topstitch to secure. Placing the mask onto Scotty's face, measure how long the elastic needs to be for a good fit; trim as required. Insert the remaining end of the elastic into the gap at the other side of the mask and topstitch in place. Fit the mask on Scotty's face.

Dougal the Dragon

🧵 🧵 🧵 Finished size: 25cm (10in) tall

Stomping around on his hind legs, whipping his powerful tail from side to side, and flapping his wings, Dougal the Dragon makes quite an impression with his bold, brightly coloured coat, spiky back and impressive red horns. But don't be fooled – there is nothing to fear. Take a closer look to see a tiny flash of a cheeky grin and you will quickly realize that his huff and puff is all for show.

Construction of this fiery fellow involves a number of toy-making techniques such as button jointing, gussets, adding ric-rac in seams and attaching small parts with ladder stitch. Although he is a little bit fiddly to make, the end result is well worth the effort.

YOU WILL NEED

Note: Buttons should be omitted if making this toy for a very small child.

* 28cm (11in) x the full width of 106–114cm (42–44in) wide blue number print fabric (body, head gusset, arms, legs)
* 30 x 10cm (12 x 4in) white spot print fabric (tummy gusset)
* 18 x 18cm (7 x 7in) red dot print fabric (wings, horns)
* 12.5 x 9cm (5 x 3½in) lightweight fusible fleece
* 50cm (20in) medium to large green ric-rac
* Four medium/large red buttons for button jointing
* Six-strand embroidery thread (floss) in colour to match buttons
* Two small black buttons for eyes
* Dollmaker's needle: 12.5cm (5in) or longer
* Good quality polyester thread
* Good quality toy filling

Cutting Your Fabrics

Note: Trace the Dragon templates (see Templates) onto tracing paper or template plastic, transferring all of the markings, and cut them out along the traced lines. When using these templates to trace the pattern pieces onto your fabric, do ensure that the marked grain line on the template matches the grain line of your fabric.

From your blue number print fabric

Fold the fabric, trace around the body template once and cut out along the traced line to give you two body pieces.

Open out the fabric and trace the head gusset template once onto single layer fabric and cut out along the traced line.

Refold the fabric and trace the arm and leg templates twice each onto the folded fabric, flipping the templates for your second trace. **Do not** cut out (these will be sewn on the traced line).

From your white spot print fabric

Trace the tummy gusset template once onto fabric and cut out along the traced line.

From your red dot-print fabric

Cut one piece measuring 12.5 x 18cm (5 x 7in) for the wings and one piece measuring 5 x 18cm (2 x 7in) for the horns.

Preparing to Start

1 Interface half of the red dot wing fabric with the fusible fleece piece, and then fold the fabric in half with right sides together, so that one side is interfaced and the other is not. Trace the wing template twice onto the interfaced side, flipping for your second trace. **Do not** cut out (these will be sewn on the traced lines).

2 Take your piece of red dot horn fabric and fold in half with right sides together. Trace around the horn template twice but **do not** cut out (these will be sewn on the traced lines).

3 Set your sewing machine to a small stitch length of approx 1.5 for stitching the toy and use a good quality polyester thread for strong seams.

Making the Dragon

Note: A 6mm (¼in) seam allowance is included in all pattern pieces unless advised otherwise. Read through all instructions before beginning to avoid surprises.

1 Place one of the body pieces right side up on your work surface. Take your ric-rac and, working from one end, pin it into position from the first star marking on the head to the second star marking near the tail. Cut and put aside the remainder of your ric-rac (this will be used in step 2). Machine tack (baste) the ric-rac into place all the way along the edge, making sure that you carefully ease your ric-rac ends to the outside of the body to start and end neatly (see Fig. 1). Snip away any excess at the ends.

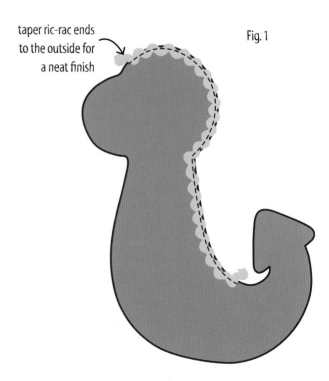

taper ric-rac ends to the outside for a neat finish

Fig. 1

TIP

When attaching ric-rac to a piece that has yet to be sewn, keep in mind the 6mm (¼in) seam allowance. Be sure to position and attach the ric-rac so that the centre of the ric-rac will be secured when sewn.

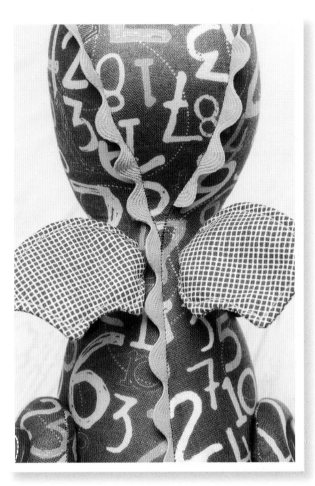

2 Attach the remaining ric-rac length in the same way to the right side of the second body piece, from the star marking at the front of the head to the dot marking at the back of the head. Machine tack (baste) in place (see Fig. 2). Snip away any excess at the ends. (Note: careful positioning of your ric-rac within the seam line will ensure a line of prominent spikes without any gaps.)

3 Take the head gusset and tummy gusset pieces and place on top of each other, right sides together, and sew together along the straight neckline edge. Press seam open.

Fig. 2

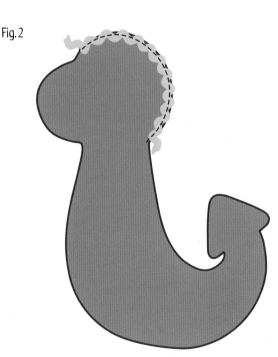

4 Take the joined head/tummy gusset piece and position it on top of one of the body pieces with right sides together as in Fig. 3: start by matching up the head/tummy gusset seam with the triangle at the front neckline as marked on the body template (a), then tack (baste) the head gusset section into place around the head to the back of the neck (b). Finally tack (baste) the tummy gusset section into place towards the tail (c). Do not pull either fabric piece but ease generously: note, the gusset will not fit the entire length to the tail – this is intentional. Once tacked (basted) in place, sew the head/gusset and body pieces together, tapering your stitching off the seam allowance at either end of the gusset strip (see Fig. 3).

Fig. 3

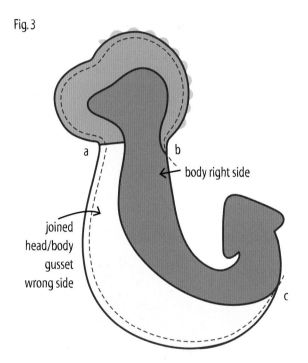

a   b

→ body right side

joined
head/body
gusset
wrong side

c

5 Now tack (baste) the remaining side of the head/tummy gusset to the remaining body piece in the same way, but leave a gap along the bottom edge for turning as indicated by the broken line on the body template and continue your tacking (basting) all the way around the back and tail to join the body pieces. Both sides of the gusset need to be evenly distributed within the body with no gathering or pulling – if you are unhappy with the fit, start again, and this time be more generous with the side that was too long.

6 Before turning the dragon through to the right side, snip the corners at the tail triangle and carefully snip the seam allowance at the front neckline. Turn right side out and then stuff the dragon firmly with toy filling. (Be sure to stuff the dragon's tail to the very ends for a nice firm shape.) Ladder stitch the opening closed (see Stitching Techniques) filling with a little more stuffing as you go to avoid a dimple.

TIP
I recommend that you ladder stitch
along both the front and back edge of
the wing, and that you go over your
stitching twice to create a strong join.

7 Take the folded piece of interfaced red dot print fabric with the wings traced onto it and, keeping the fabric folded, sew along the traced lines, leaving the straight ends unstitched as indicated by the broken line on the wing template. Cut out the wings approx 3mm (⅛in) outside the sewn lines, and then turn the wings right side out. Press well, and then topstitch all the way around the wings, turning under the open edges to neaten in the process.

8 Take one of the wings and using strong polyester thread, take small hand running stitches along the straight edge; pull up the thread to slightly gather the edge and continue with the same thread to attach the wing in position on the dragon's back with ladder stitch. (Refer to photographs for a guide to positioning and Stitching Techniques for how to work ladder stitch.) Repeat to secure the second wing in place.

9 Take the folded piece of red dot print fabric with the horns traced onto it and, keeping the fabric folded, sew along the traced lines, leaving the straight ends unstitched as indicated by the broken line on the horn template. Cut out the horns approx 3mm (⅛in) outside the sewn lines, then turn right side out. Fold in the raw edges by approx 6mm (¼in) and finger press to give a neat edge, and then stuff each horn firmly with toy filling.

10 Position a horn at one side of the dragon's head gusset, referring to the photographs as a guide to positioning. Hold the horn in place by pinning through the horn and into the head, much like a pin cushion. Using strong polyester thread, ladder stitch the horn in place working in a circle (see Stitching Techniques: Attaching Parts). When you get approx three quarters of the way around, stuff the horn a little bit more to make sure it is nice and firm. I recommend you stitch around at least twice to ensure the horn is firmly attached. Repeat to place and secure the second horn.

TIP

If you are making this toy for a baby
or a small child, omit the buttons and
blanket stitch a small piece of black
wool felt in place or create the eyes
with satin stitch.

11 Using black thread, sew the small black button eyes into place on the dragon's face. Pull the thread to indent the eyes ever so slightly if desired.

12 Take the folded piece of body fabric with the legs and arms traced onto it and, keeping the fabric folded, sew all the way around the traced lines. Cut the pieces out approx 3–6mm (⅛– ¼in) outside your sewn line. Do not snip the seams. To turn the limbs right side out, cut the small turning slit as marked on the arm and leg templates on **one side only** of each limb (single fabric thickness).

TIP

Make certain you cut a slit into
the correct fabric layer so that you
are creating two mirror image
arms and legs.

13 Stuff each limb firmly with toy filling, then whip stitch the opening closed (see Stitching Techniques). As the turning gaps will be hidden against the dragon's body, there is no need to worry about perfect stitching. It is important to stuff the legs very firmly so that they can support the toy's weight.

14 The button jointing technique is used to attach the limbs to the dragon's body and you should start by attaching the legs. First thread the dollmaker's needle with a long length (approx 150cm/60in) of six-strand embroidery thread (floss) in a colour to match your buttons. Tie a double knot in the end of your length of thread and trim close to the knot.

15 Referring to Fig. 4, begin button jointing. Start by threading the needle through one side of the dragon's body at the desired leg location (refer to the photographs), taking it right through the body and out the other side at exactly the same level. Thread the needle through one of the legs, then through one of the buttons, then go back through all of the layers again (button, leg, body) to come back out close to your start point. Here, thread the needle through the remaining leg and button, as shown in Fig. 4, and return again through the body to the other side. Continue through all the layers a few times, for a nice strong attachment, pulling the threads taut after each pass through. Tie off your thread and sink the knot into the leg (see Stitching Techniques).

16 Repeat the button jointing process to attach the arms, referring to the photographs as a guide to positioning.

Fig. 4

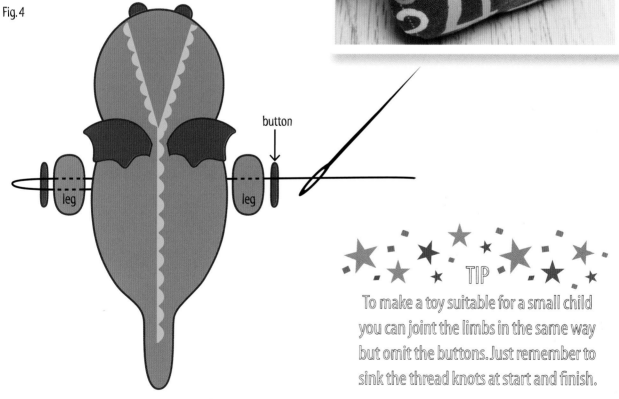

button

leg   leg

To make a toy suitable for a small child you can joint the limbs in the same way but omit the buttons. Just remember to sink the thread knots at start and finish.

Princess Penelope

Finished size: 40.5cm (16in) tall

With her lily-white complexion, you could be forgiven for thinking that Princess Penelope spends her days cooped up in the palace, but nothing could be further from the truth. There is nothing she likes better than bug hunting in the palace gardens – she keeps her hair in plaits and her gown short so she can run around with ease. She is a firm believer that just because she's a princess she doesn't have to behave like one!

Construction of Penelope requires a little patience as there are quite a few different steps to complete, but stay focused and you'll find she comes to life in no time. As everything apart from the crown is securely sewn into seams, she'd make a perfect companion for even the youngest princess.

YOU WILL NEED

* 15cm (6in) x the full width of 106–114cm (42–44in) wide pink floral print fabric (hair, peplum)
* 25 x 35cm (10 x 14in) blue patterned fabric (body, shoes)
* 10 x 56cm (4 x 22in) red patterned fabric (skirt)
* 23cm (9in) x the full width of 106–114cm (42–44in) wide natural cotton/linen blend fabric (head, arms, legs)
* 12.5 x 10cm (5 x 4in) yellow wool felt (crown)
* 2.5 x 2.5cm (1 x 1in) red wool felt (heart decoration)
* 25cm (10in) of small white ric-rac
* 15 x 18cm (6 x 7in) fusible web
* Six-strand embroidery thread (floss): black, pink, blue
* Good quality polyester thread
* Good quality toy filling

Cutting Your Fabrics

Note: Trace the Princess templates (see Templates) onto tracing paper or template plastic, transferring all the markings, and cut them out along the traced lines. When using these templates to trace the pattern pieces onto your fabric, do ensure that the marked grain line on the template matches the grain line of your fabric.

From your pink floral print fabric

Cut six strips each measuring 3.25 x 18cm (1¼ x 7in) for the plaits.

Cut one piece measuring 15 x 25cm (6 x 10in) for the skirt peplum.

Trace the head template once and cut out on the traced line for the head back.

From your blue patterned fabric

Cut one strip measuring 7.5 x 30.5cm (3 x 12in) for the shoes.

Fold the fabric and trace around the body top and body bottom templates once; cut out along the traced lines to give you two body tops and two body bottoms.

From your red patterned fabric

Cut one strip measuring 10 x 56cm (4 x 22in) for the skirt.

From your natural cotton/linen blend fabric

Cut one strip measuring 15 x 30.5cm (6 x 12in) for the legs.

Trace the head template once and cut out on the traced line.

Fold the remaining fabric in half and trace around the arm template twice, but **do not** cut out (these will be sewn on the traced line).

Preparing to Start

1 Trace the hairline template onto the paper side of the fusible web, rough cut out close to the traced line and then fuse this to the wrong side of your remaining pink floral print. Cut the hair shape out along the traced line and then fuse this to your natural cotton/linen blend head piece. This is the head front.

2 Take the pink floral print fabric for the skirt peplum, fold in half right sides together, and trace around the peplum template twice but **do not** cut out. Put aside for now.

3 Trace the heart shape from the crown template onto the paper side of the fusible web and rough cut out. Fuse the heart to the red felt, cut along the traced line and put aside for now.

4 Set your sewing machine to a small stitch length of approx 1.5 for stitching the toy and use a good quality polyester thread for strong seams.

Making the Princess

Note: A 6mm (¼in) seam allowance is included in all pattern pieces unless advised otherwise. Read through all the instructions before starting to avoid surprises.

1 Machine appliqué the hairline into place on the head front (I used a small machine blanket stitch).

2 Cut your length of white ric-rac in half. Taking one of the body top pieces, place the ric-rac along the neckline with the right side facing you and machine tack (baste) into place stitching within the seam allowance, approx 3mm (⅛in) from the raw edge. Attach the remaining ric-rac length to the second body top piece in the same way.

4 Take one of your pink floral print fabric plait strips, fold in one short end by approx 6mm (¼in) and press well. Fold the strip in half lengthways, with wrong sides together, and press. Open out and fold the raw edges of each long edge evenly to the fold line and press along the fold line once again, topstitching the strip along the open edge to secure (see Fig. 1). Repeat to prepare the remaining five plait strips.

5 Take three of your prepared plait strips and partially overlapping, secure the raw ends together with a few machine stitches close to the edge. Lay the joined body/head front piece right side up on your work surface and place the three joined plait strips onto the head so that they lay diagonally across the face (see Fig. 2 for placement) and machine tack (baste) into position. Repeat with the remaining strips on the other side of the head.

Carefully position your ric-rac within the seam line to ensure a pretty line of trim at Penelope's neckline without any gaps.

3 Take one of the body top pieces and the head front with hair and place on top of each other, right sides together. Ensuring that the placement is central, ease the neckline of the body to the neckline of the head, pinning or tacking (basting) into place before sewing together. Repeat to join the pink floral print head back to the remaining body top piece.

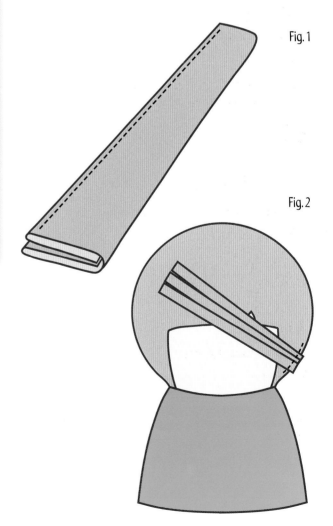

Fig. 1

Fig. 2

6 Take your folded linen with the arms traced onto it and, keeping the fabric folded, sew along the traced lines of the arms, leaving the straight ends unstitched as indicated by the broken line on the template. Cut out the arms approx 3mm (⅛in) outside your sewn lines, and then turn the arms right side out.

7 Firmly stuff the arms with toy filling, leaving the last 2cm (¾in) unstuffed. Make small running stitches around the top raw edges of each arm, pulling the thread to gather; secure with tacking (basting) stitches.

8 With the body/head front still right side up on your work surface, place each arm in turn at the top of the body so the raw edges align (see Fig. 3) and machine tack (baste) in place. Make sure to position the arms as shown in Fig. 3, with the thumbs on the outside – when the doll is complete all will be well and the hands will be the right way around.

Fig. 3

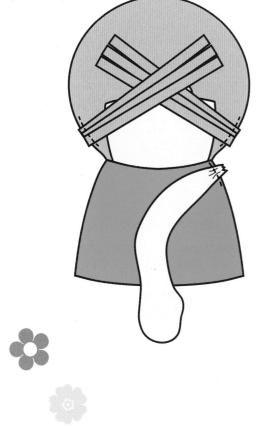

9 Take the body/head back and place it on top of the body/head front, right sides together. Pin or tack (baste) these two pieces together ensuring that the neckline seams align and that the plait strips and arms remain clear of your stitching. When you are happy with the fit, sew the pieces together leaving the bottom edge open. Turn through to the right side.

10 Take your red patterned fabric skirt strip and fold it in half, right sides together, so that the short ends meet, and sew in place to make your skirt ring; press the seam open. Neaten one long edge of the skirt ring with a narrow double hem: fold under the raw edge by approx 6mm (¼in) and press in place, then fold under again to create a neat edge and press once more before topstitching in place.

11 Take your folded pink floral print fabric with the peplums traced onto it and, keeping the fabric folded, sew along the traced lines, leaving the top section open as indicated by the broken line on the peplum template. Cut the peplums out approx 3mm (⅛in) outside your sewn line and turn right side out; press and then topstitch along the sewn edges.

12 Return to your main skirt ring and mark the halfway points along the top raw edge only. Take one of your peplum pieces and centre the top raw edge along one of the halfway points on the skirt ring as shown in Fig. 4, and machine tack (baste) in place. Repeat to attach the remaining peplum to the other halfway point on the skirt.

Fig. 4

machine tack (baste) peplums to
top edge of skirt ring

13 The skirt will be gathered to fit, so you need to work two lines of machine stitching at approx 3mm (⅛in) and 6mm (¼in) from the top raw edge of your skirt (including peplums). Begin by setting your machine to the largest stitch size and make sure not to secure your stitching at the start and finish.

14 Once both stitching lines have been worked, pull the loose bobbin threads to gather the top skirt edge evenly. You are aiming for this to measure the same circumference as the open end of Penelope's body (approx 24cm/9½in). Adjust your gathers so that the peplums sit nicely and evenly at either side. (I chose to have the peplum sections only very slightly gathered and the front and back skirt sections more heavily gathered.)

15 Fit the gathered skirt over the open end of the body so that right sides are together and the raw gathered edge of the skirt is lined up with the raw bottom edge of the body. Tack (baste) neatly and evenly in place.

16 Take the two body bottom pieces and sew along the short edges with right sides together to create a ring. Keeping the fabric ring inside out, fit the body bottom over the skirt so that what will become the top edge of the body bottom meets the raw edge of the body/skirt layers. Tack (baste) in place. Remembering to re-set your machine stitch to a small stitch length of approx 1.5, sew these three layers together securely. Fold the skirt and body bottom down into place.

17 To make Penelope's legs, start by making your leg panel fabric: take the linen leg strip and blue patterned fabric shoe strip and sew with right sides together along one long 30.5cm (12in) edge. Open out and press. Fold the fabric panel in half width ways, so that the short edges meet and right sides are together, making sure that the fabrics and seam line are perfectly aligned.

18 Place the leg template onto the folded fabric panel making sure that the marked shoe line matches up with the seam in the fabric. Draw around it twice, flipping the template for the second trace. Keeping the fabric panel folded, sew along the traced lines, leaving the straight ends unstitched as indicated by the broken line on the template. Cut out each leg approx 3mm (⅛in) outside your sewn lines and turn the legs right side out. Firmly stuff the limbs to the very ends with toy filling, leaving the last 2.5cm (1in) unstuffed. Tack (baste) the open ends closed.

19 Fold the bottom edge of the body in by 6mm (¼in) and press in place. Take the legs and, ensuring that the toes are facing inwards, position them between the folded edges of the body so that the left leg is at the left side seam and the right leg is at the right side seam, and tack (baste) in place. There should be a gap between the legs as in Fig. 5. Topstitch the legs into place as close to the body edge as possible and through all layers, leaving the gap between the legs open for stuffing.

Fig. 5

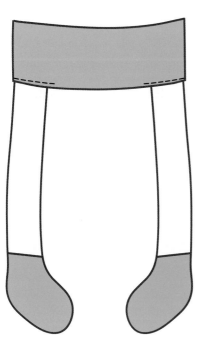

20 Now stuff Penelope with toy filling: stuff the head first ensuring that you have a firm fill before starting to stuff the body. When the head and body are firmly stuffed, ladder stitch the opening closed, stuffing a little more as you go if required.

21 Plait the fabric strips at either side of the head and secure the ends of the plaits with a few stitches. Cover the securing stitches with a bow tied from two lengths of all six strands of blue embroidery thread (floss).

22 Mark the facial details onto Penelope's face (see head template). Using two strands of pink embroidery thread (floss) create the mouth with backstitch and the cheek circles with running stitch. Using two strands of black embroidery thread (floss), satin stitch the eyes and backstitch the eyelashes.

TIP

If you are intending to give this toy to a baby or very young child, omit the crown as this small part could be a choking hazard.

23 To make Penelope's crown, take the piece of yellow felt and fold it in half. Trace the crown template onto the folded felt and then cut out to give you two crown pieces. Pin the crown pieces together so that they are aligned, and topstitch together all the way around them, as close to the edge as possible. Fuse the red felt heart to the centre front of the crown and appliqué in place with standard straight stitch. Fold the crown in half, right sides together, so the short ends meet and sew with a 3mm (⅛in) seam allowance. Turn right side out.

24 Position the crown as desired onto the princess's head and pin in place. Using two strands of strong polyester thread, ladder stitch the bottom edge of the crown into place (see Stitching Techniques: Attaching Parts), going around your stitching at least twice to ensure a strong attachment.

TIP

I chose to position my doll's crown off to one side of the head as she is always running around, but you could place yours centrally if you prefer.

Stitching Techniques

For the strongest possible stitching, sew your toy pieces together with machine stitching. You will also need a few simple hand-sewing stitches to finish off and bring your toy designs to life.

Machine sewing

For all sewing of the body pieces for the toys, set the stitch length on your sewing machine to 1.5 and use good quality strong polyester thread. For the sewing of clothing, set the stitch length to 2.5. Lock your stitching by starting and ending machine sewing with a few reverse stitches. This ensures that the seam won't split when you are turning and stuffing your soft toys.

Some of the toy body pieces require stitching along the marked outline before cutting out, while others have a 6mm (¼in) seam allowance allowed in the pattern pieces. Therefore, make sure that you read the full instructions for making each toy before you begin.

Hand sewing

Although the toys are mostly machine stitched, there are times when you will need to hand stitch, when sewing up turning gaps or adding facial details for example. All the stitches you are likely to need are explained here.

Backstitch

Backstitch creates a continuous line of stitching, so it is ideal for creating facial features on your toys.

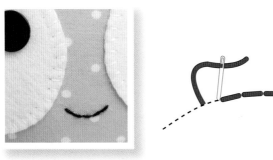

Running stitch

This simple stitch is used for gathering, as on Fifi's fairy skirt or for adding features, such as Milo's cheeks.

Blanket stitch

This is used to secure appliquéd fabric pieces.

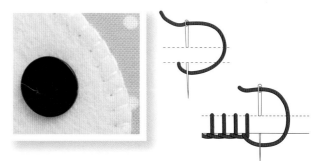

Satin stitch

This can be used to substitute for buttons if making your toy for a small child. First, backstitch the shape; then work satin stitch over the backstitch shape.

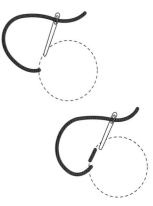

Chain stitch

Chain stitch is great for creating thicker lines and therefore perfect for embroidering Otis's long, smiling mouth, as shown here.

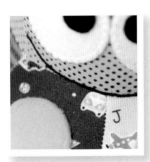 

Whip stitch

This is used to sew together the edges of a gap where the stitching won't be seen, for example to close the turning slits on the dragon's limbs.

Sinking a knot

When button jointing legs, or completing any stitching on a toy that is already stuffed, you will want to avoid any knots being visible where you start and end your stitching, so for a neat finish you will need to sink your knot into the toy. When you have completed the required sewing, tie a knot in the thread close to where it exits the toy. Take one last stitch into the toy, taking your needle through to an inconspicuous area approx 2.5–5cm (1–2in) away. Pull the thread through and it will snag when the knot reaches the fabric where you started your stitch. Hold the thread firmly and tug it quickly so that the knot pops into the toy. Snip the thread end away where it exits the fabric so that it, too, sinks into the toy.

Ladder stitch

Closing gaps

Use ladder stitch to sew turning gaps closed in a neat, strong and nearly invisible way.

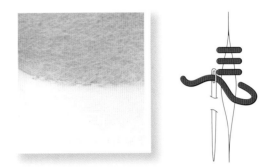

Attaching parts

Ladder stitch is also used to attach parts to soft toys. This method is usually used so that the attachment will either sit flat against or protrude from the stuffed toy. Follow the ladder stitch diagram for closing gaps, but make one stitch in the edge of the attachment, then make the next stitch in the body of the toy. The ladder stitches need to be sewn into the body following the shape of the attachment so that the attached part retains its shape.

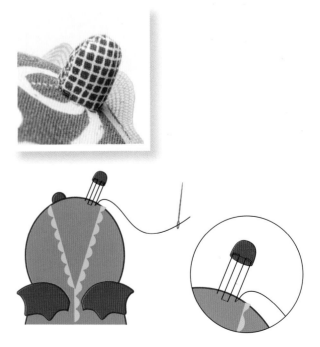

Stuffing Techniques

★ It is essential to stuff your toys very firmly, and you will be surprised at how much filling they need. As you will have sewn the seams with small stitches using strong polyester thread, they will be robust enough to withstand a large amount of stuffing. So when you think that your toy is fully stuffed, keep on stuffing: don't be scared to use large wads of filling as this will give your finished toy more structure.

★ **Using your paintbrush tool:** To prepare a round paintbrush as a stuffing tool, trim the bristles to 6–13mm (¼–½in) long. Play with the remaining bristles using your fingers and rub them against a hard surface until you have messed them up thoroughly. Shaggy bristles are desirable as they will grip onto your filling firmly and stay adhered, allowing you to easily manoeuvre it into your toy. This will also enable you to position the filling where you want it and to keep stuffing it right to the end of the toy pieces until they are super-firm.

Templates

All templates are actual size.

Alien

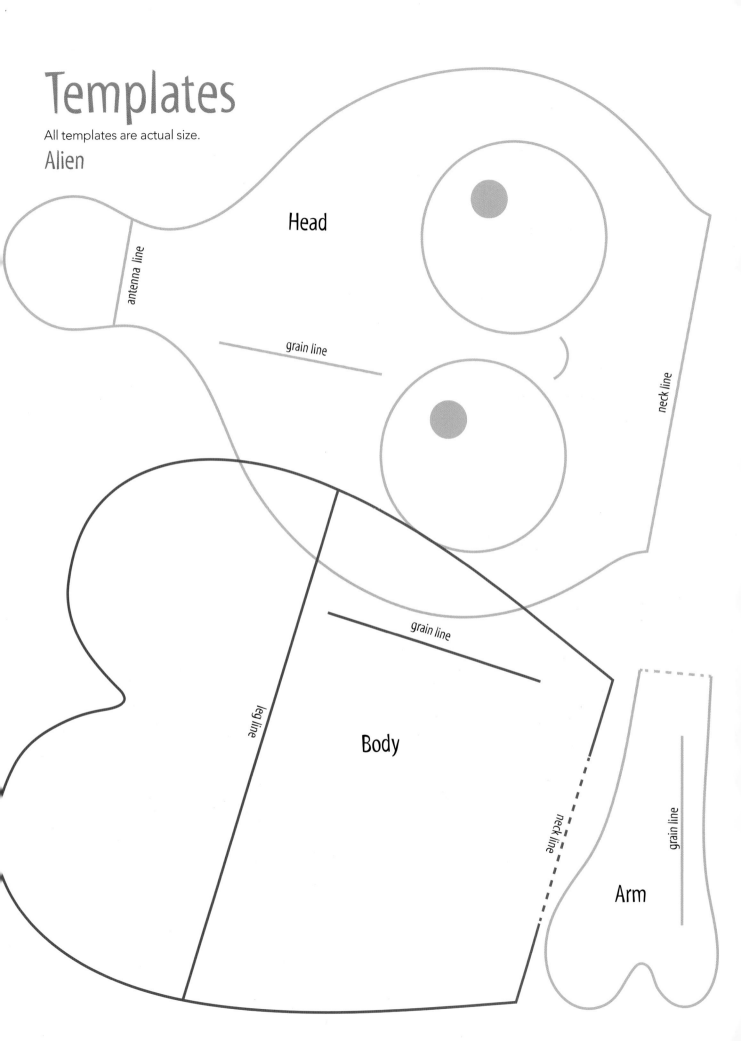

Head

antenna line

grain line

neck line

grain line

leg line

Body

neck line

grain line

Arm

UFO

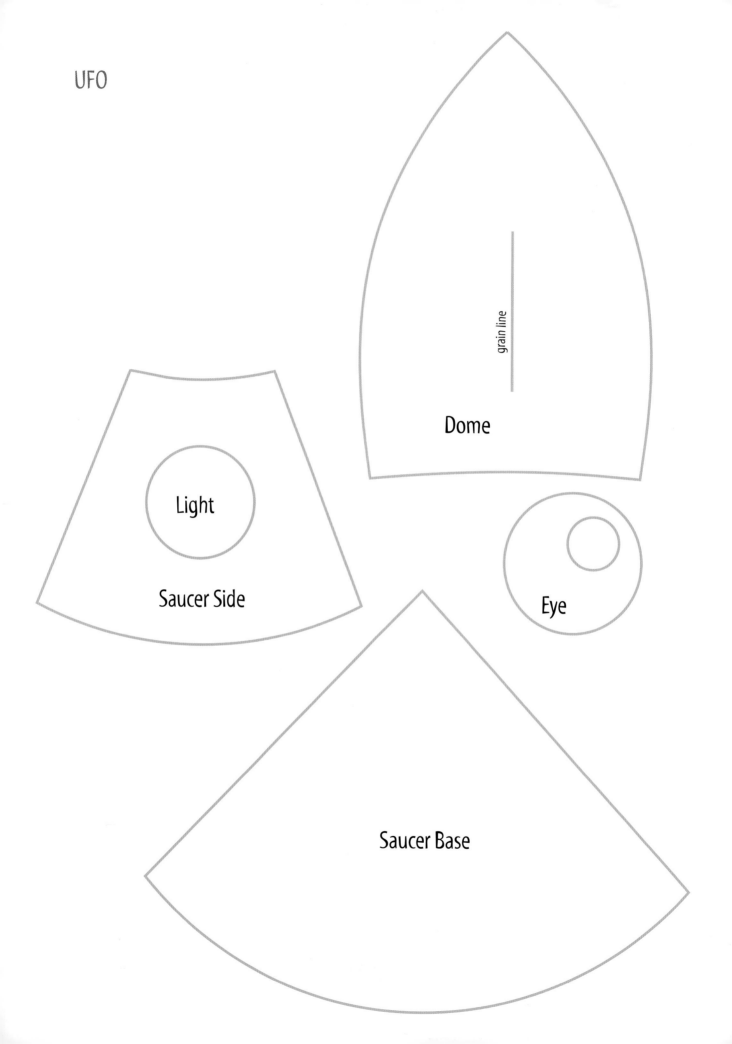

Dome

grain line

Light

Saucer Side

Eye

Saucer Base

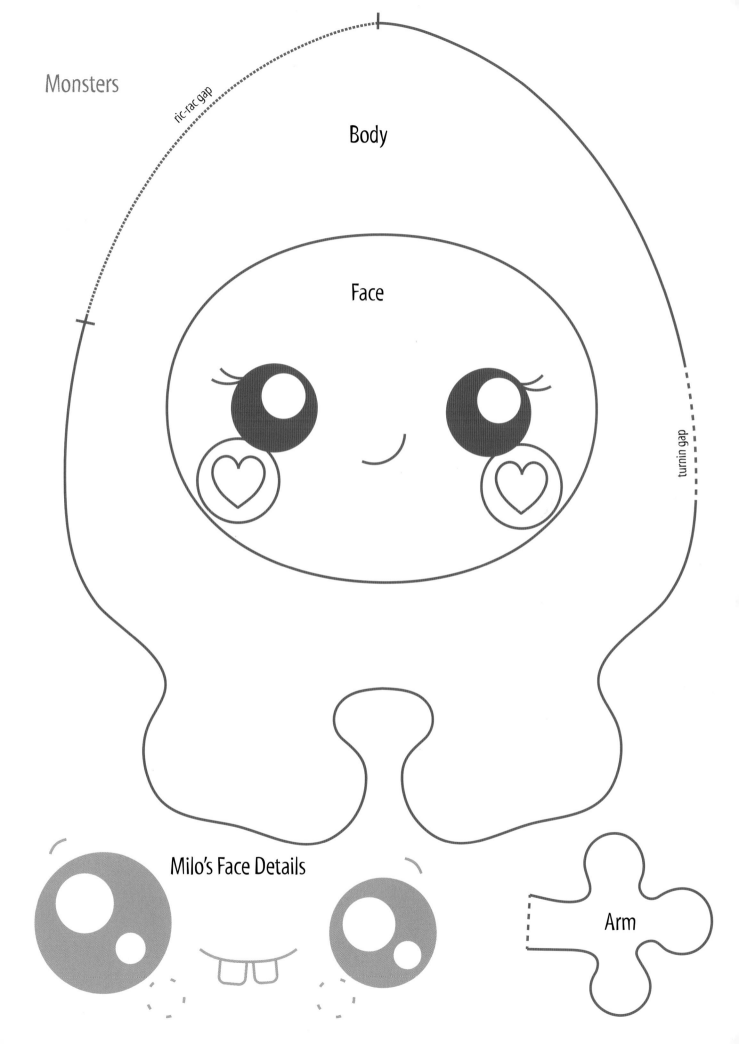

Monsters

Body

Face

ric-rac gap

turnin gap

Milo's Face Details

Arm

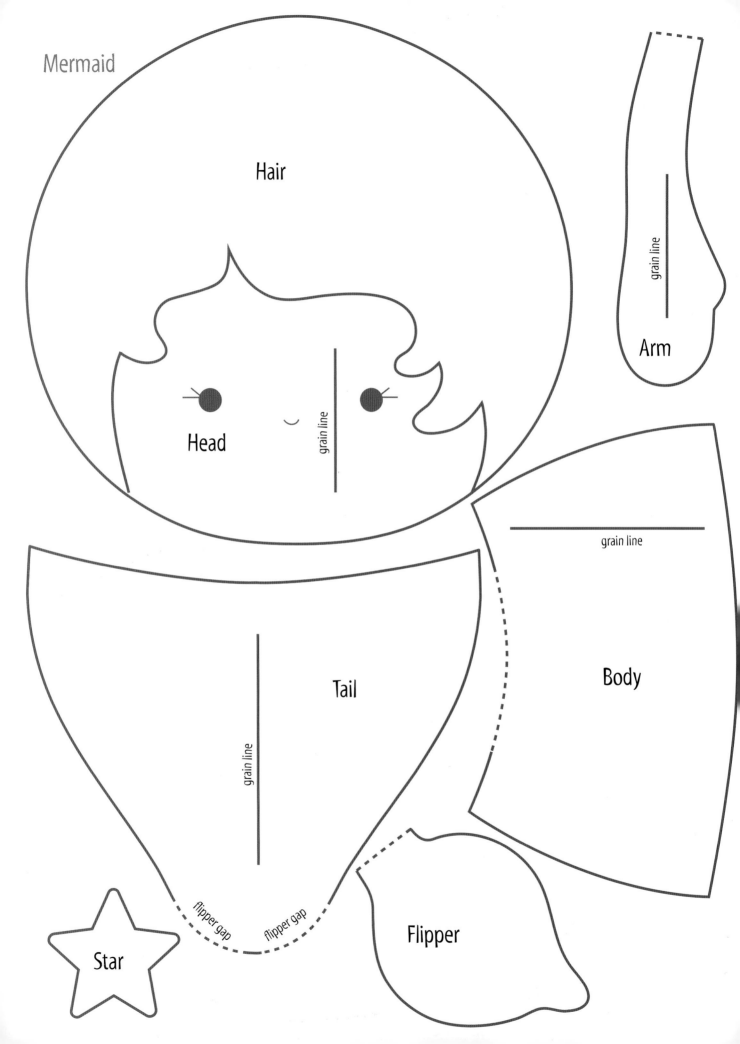

Mermaid

Hair

Head

grain line

Arm

grain line

Body

grain line

Tail

grain line

Star

flipper gap   flipper gap

Flipper

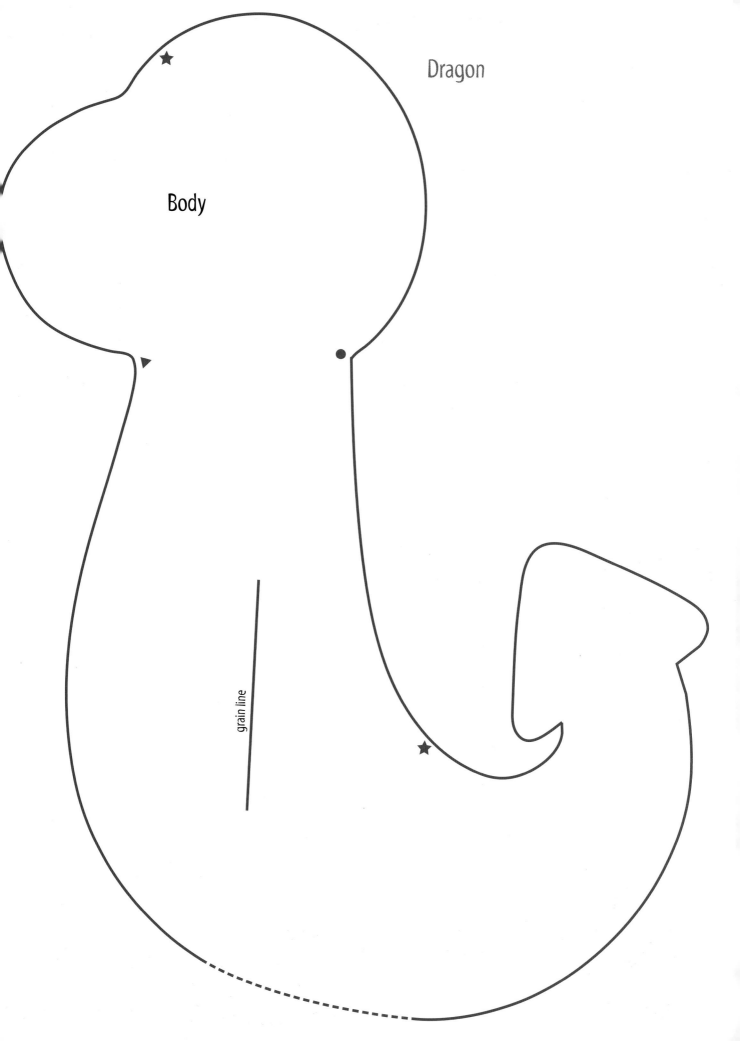

Dragon

Body

grain line

Dragon

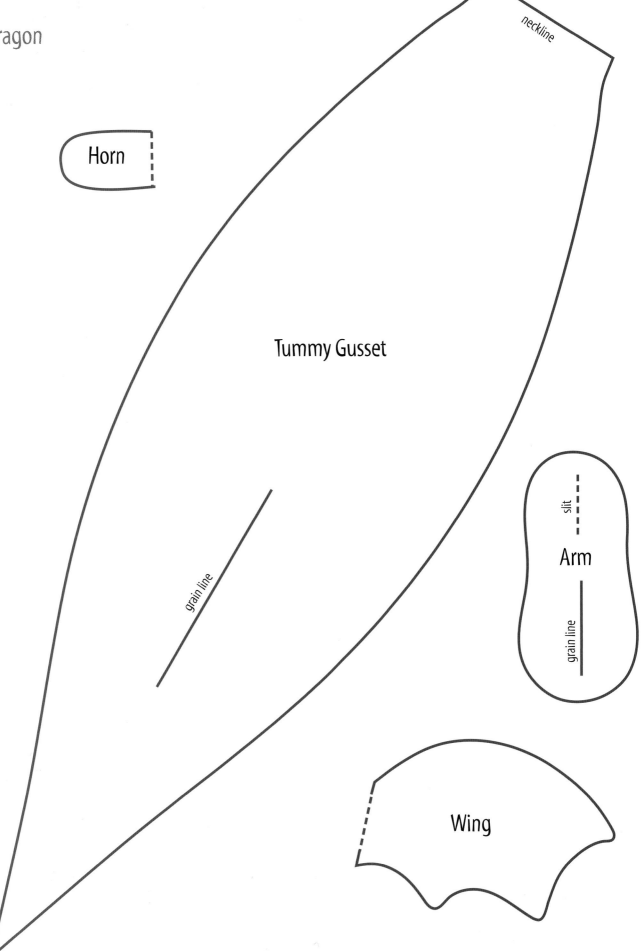

Horn

Tummy Gusset

grain line

Arm

slit

grain line

Wing

neckline

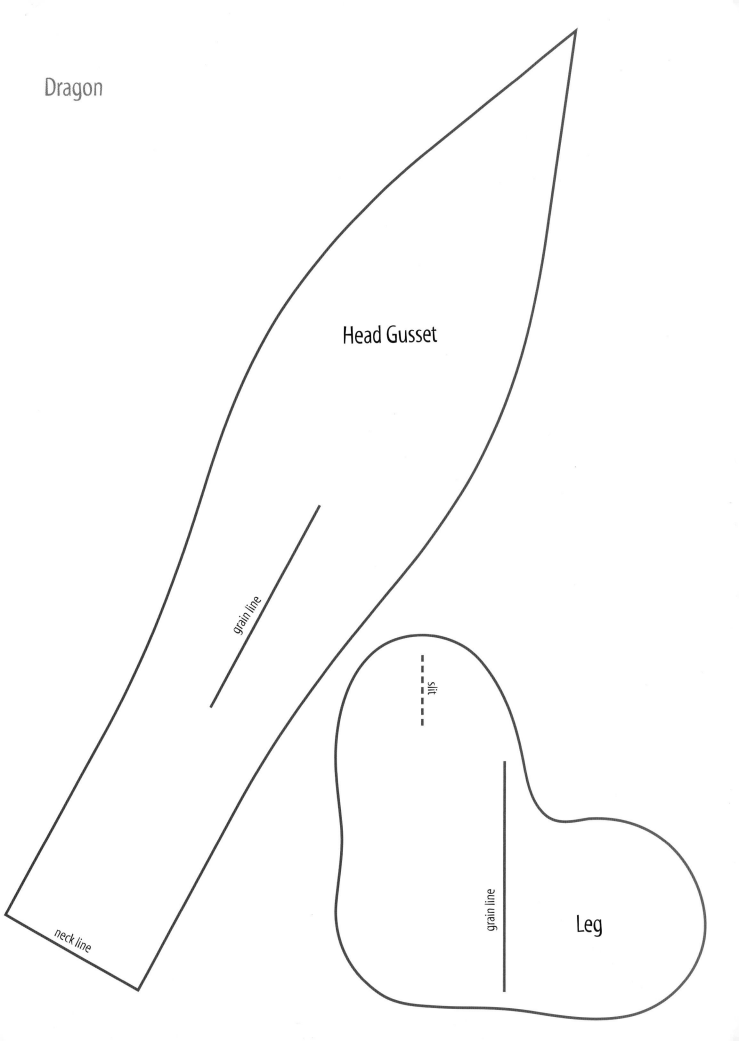

Dragon

Head Gusset

grain line

neck line

slit

grain line

Leg

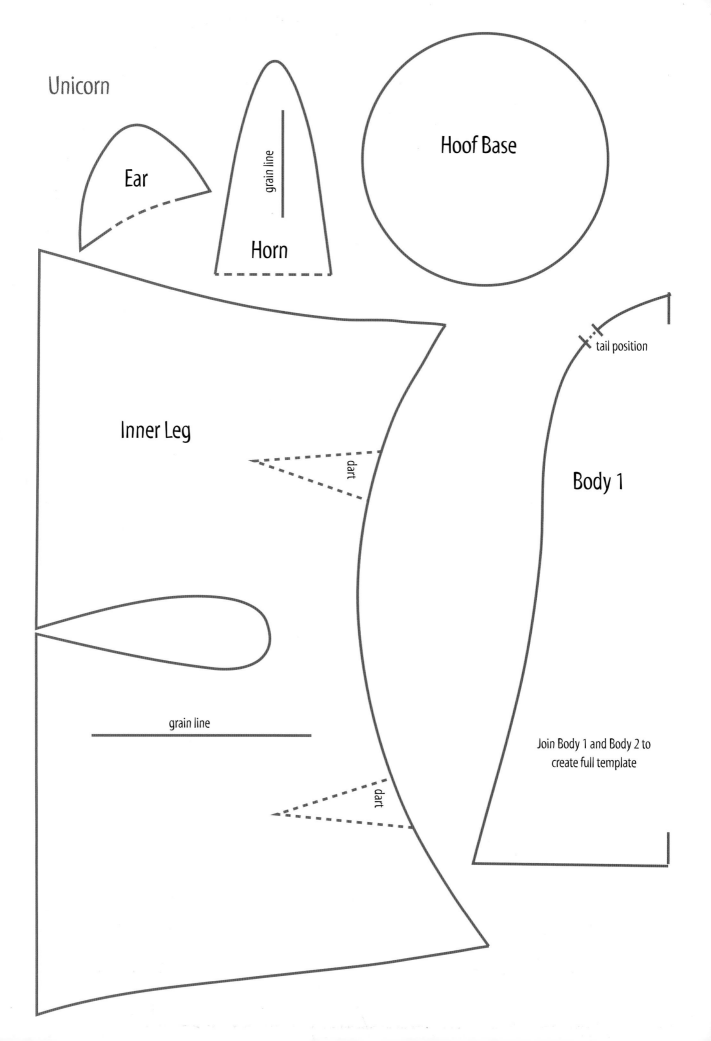

Unicorn

Ear

Horn

grain line

Hoof Base

Inner Leg

tail position

dart

Body 1

grain line

dart

Join Body 1 and Body 2 to
create full template

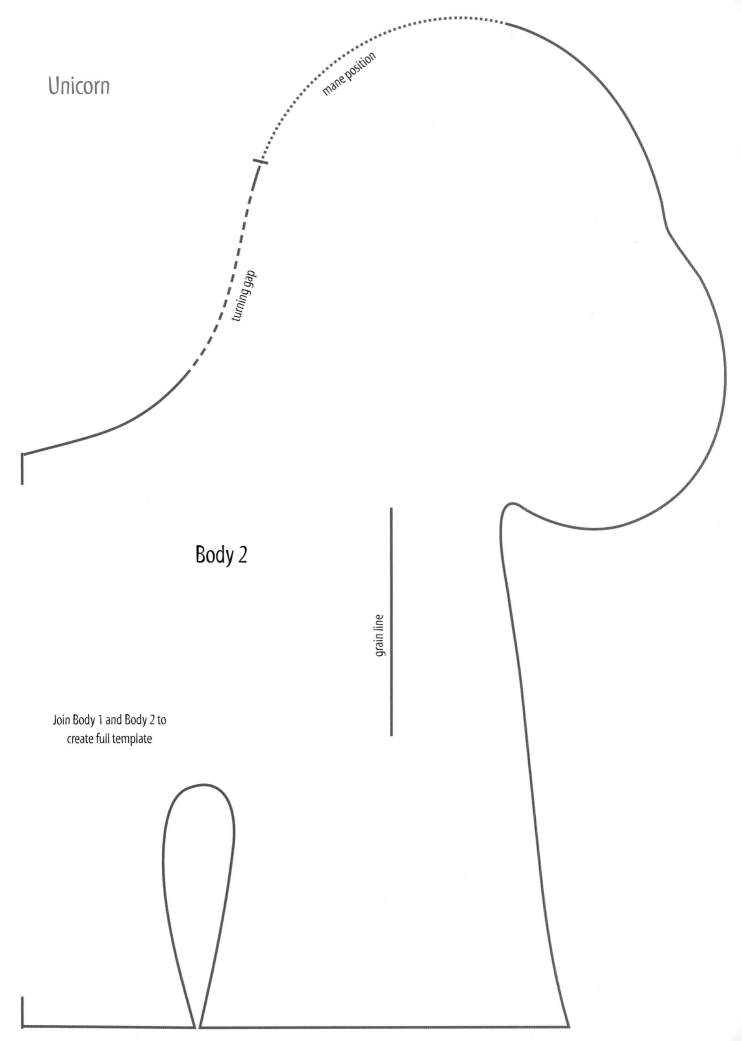

Unicorn

mane position

turning gap

Body 2

grain line

Join Body 1 and Body 2 to
create full template

Fairy

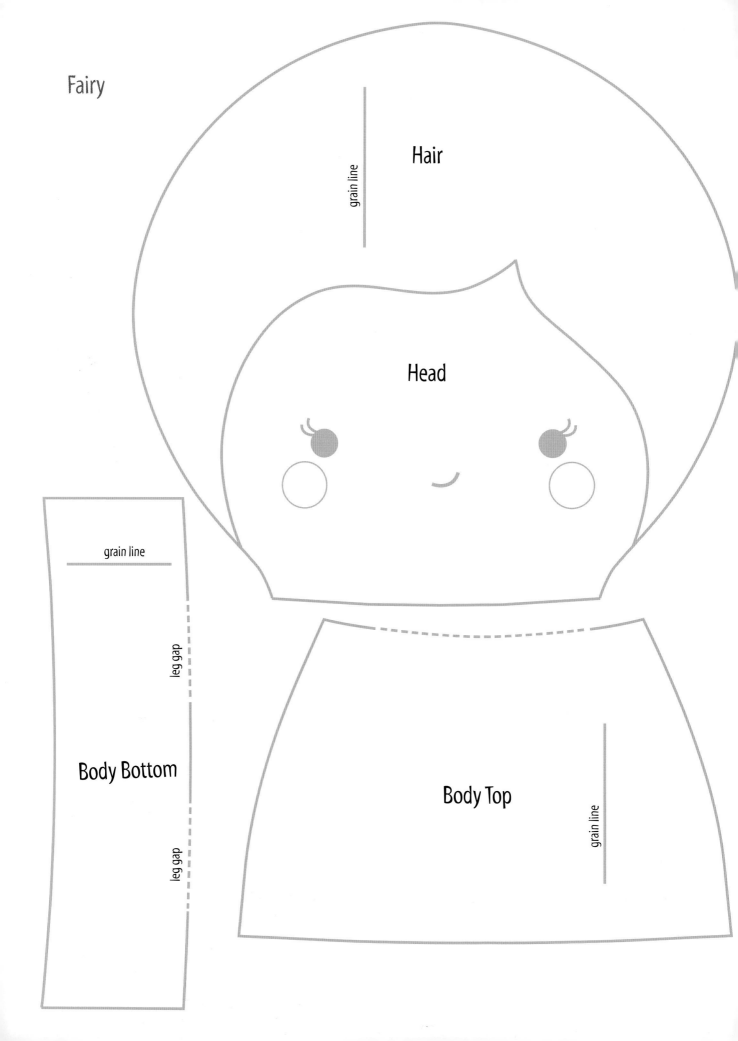

Hair

grain line

Head

grain line

Body Bottom

leg gap

leg gap

Body Top

grain line

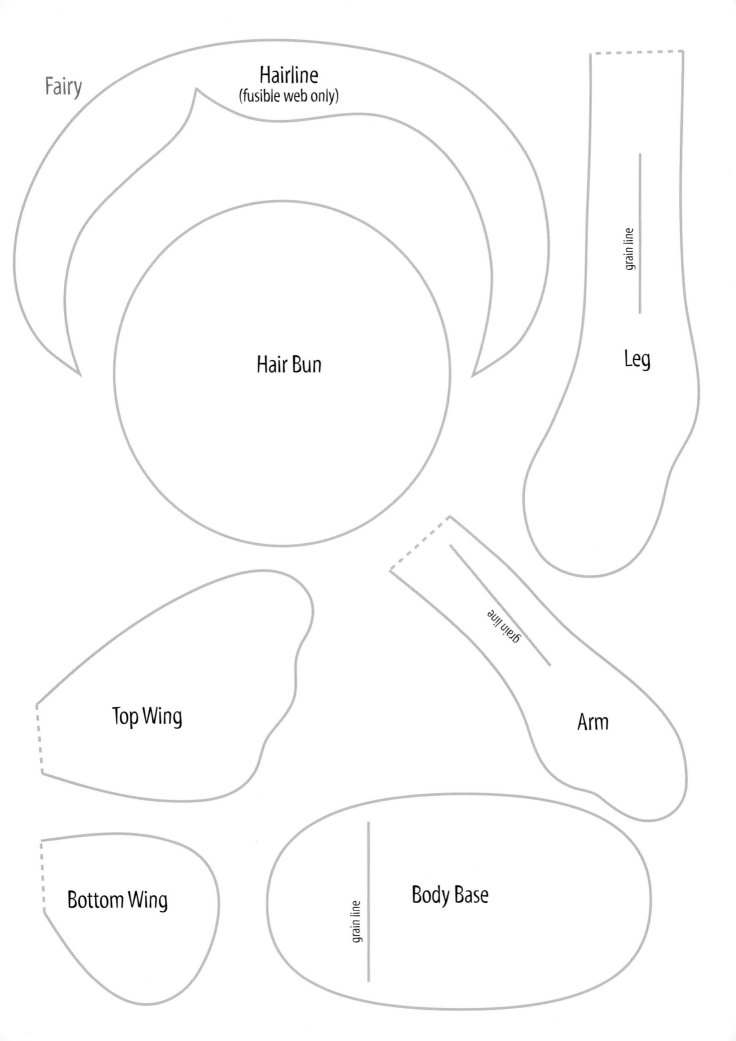

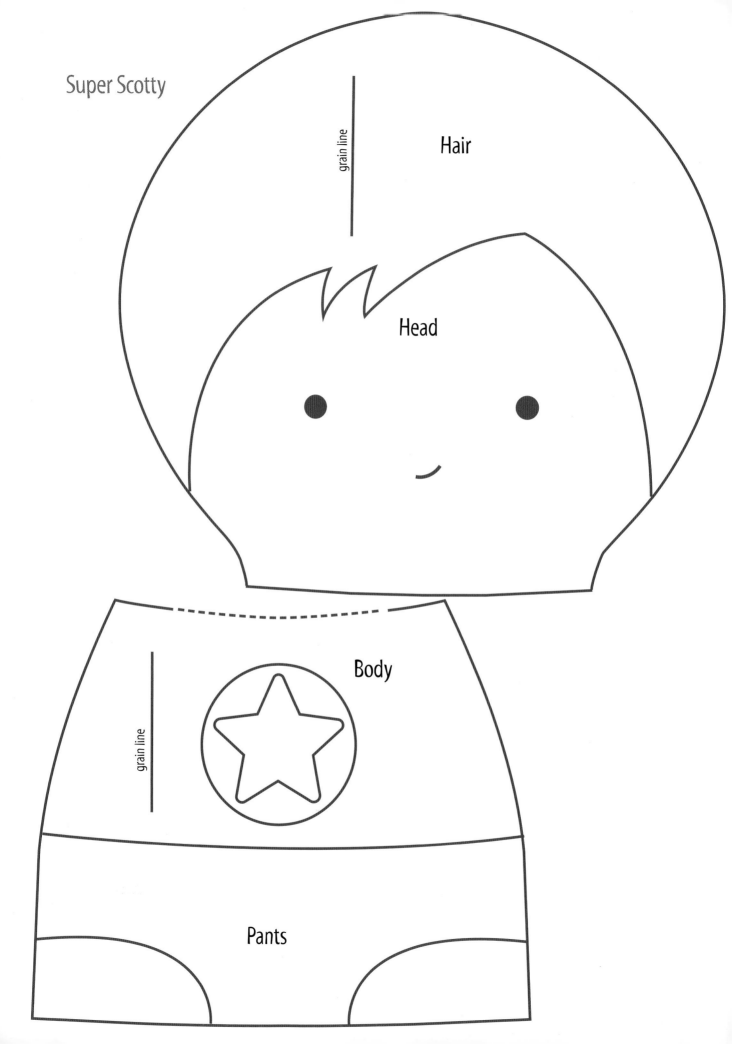

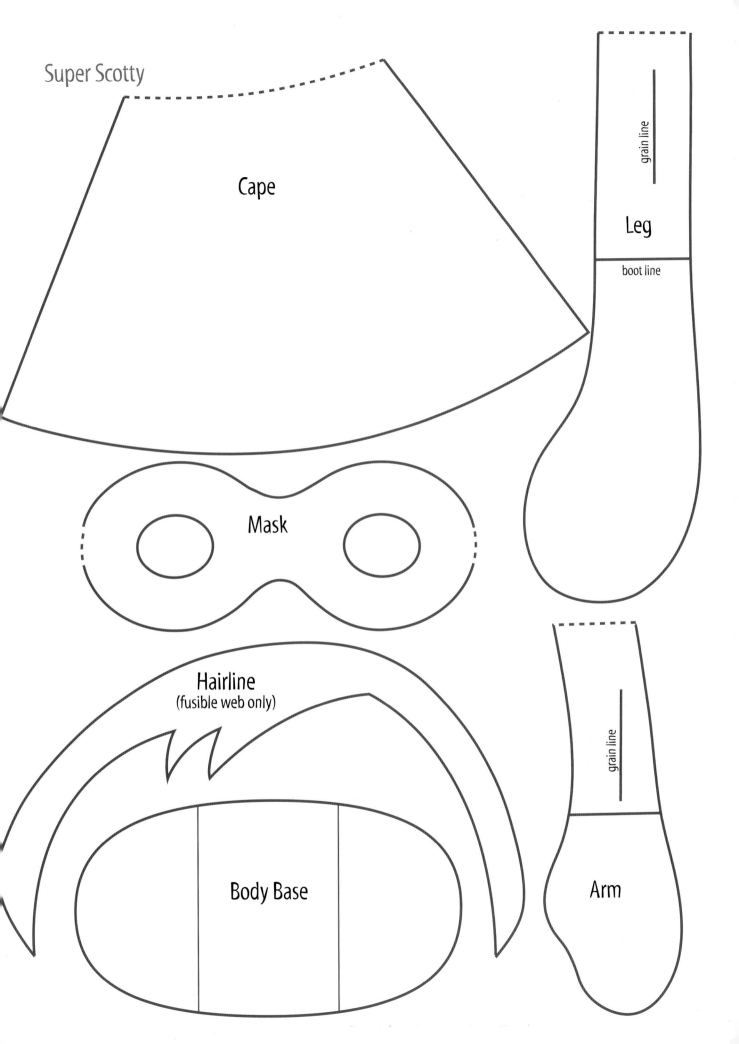

Super Scotty

Cape

Leg

grain line

boot line

Mask

Hairline
(fusible web only)

Body Base

Arm

grain line

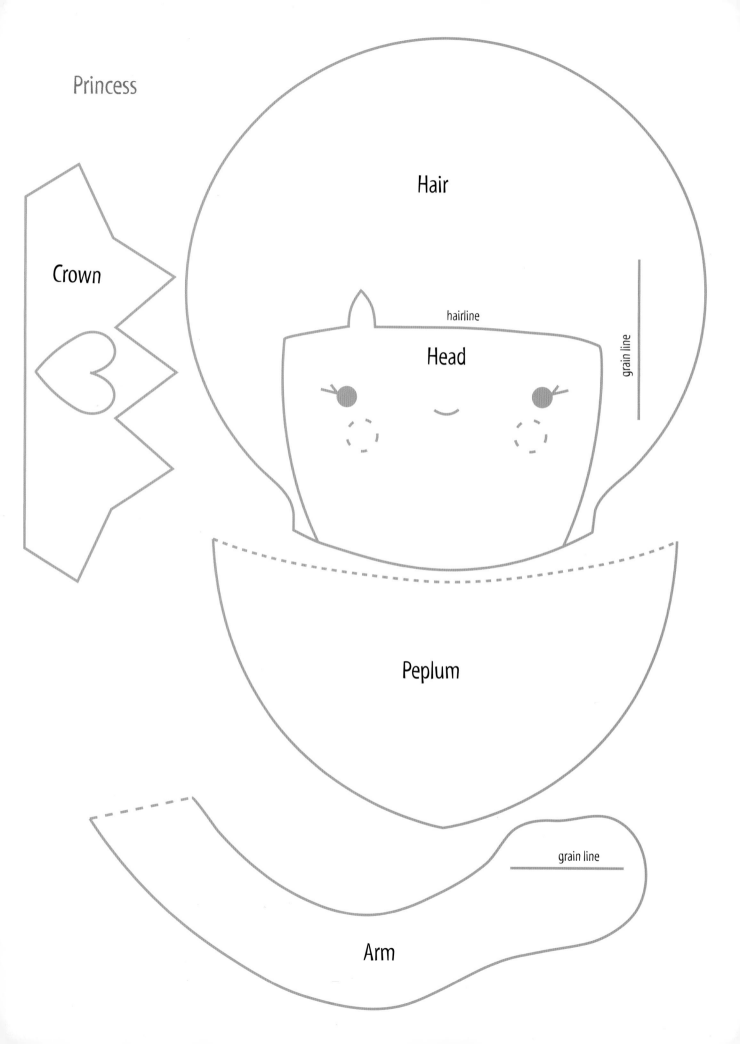

Princess

Crown

Hair

hairline

Head

grain line

Peplum

grain line

Arm

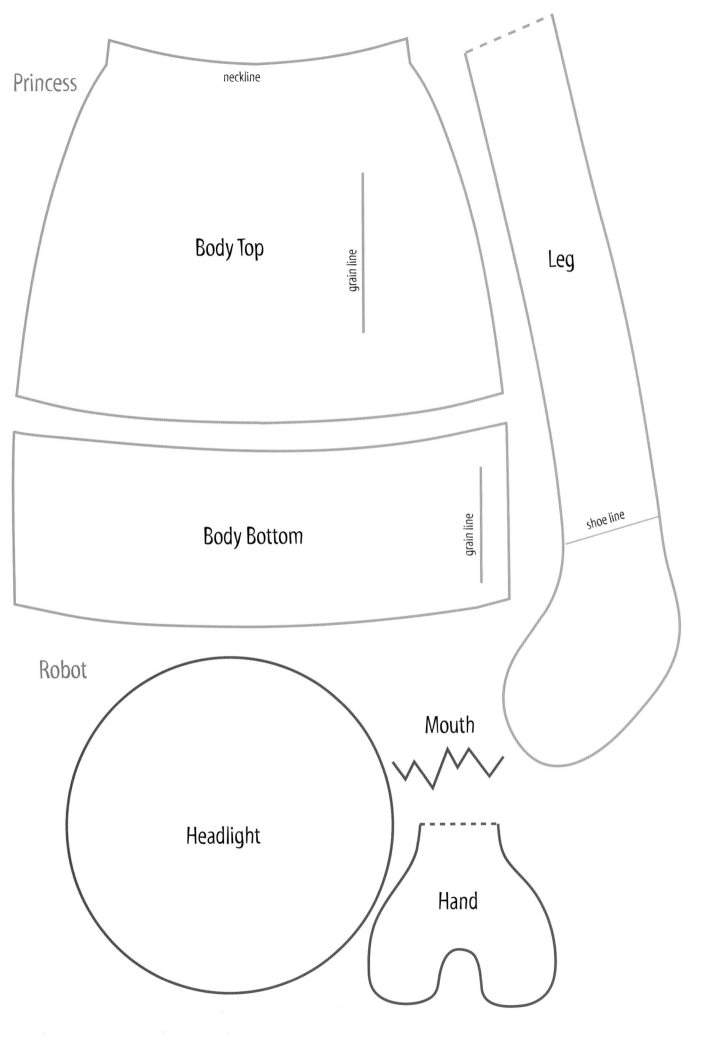

Princess

neckline

Body Top

grain line

Leg

Body Bottom

grain line

shoe line

Robot

Headlight

Mouth

Hand

About the Author

Melanie McNeice is an Aussie pattern designer based in the leafy outskirts of Melbourne, Australia. Melly's adventures in sewing began a little more than a decade ago after she found herself a stay-at-home mum with the desire to still be productive. Melly's passion for sewing grew quickly after her sister encouraged her to give it a try, and only 12 months after beginning to sew, she tried her hand at design under the pattern label Melly & me.

Melly's goals in design are to create a range of contemporary sewing patterns that include bright and quirky toys, wearable purses, as well as fun and modern quilts. Melanie aims to design items that are original and, achievable in a day, as well as being completely usable in everyday life! Melly & me has grown to appeal to a worldwide audience, and Melly has designed in excess of 100 patterns, published five books, *Kaleidoscope*, *Sewn Toy Tales*, *Snug as a Bug*, *Sew Cute to Carry* and *Fun of the Fair*, and teaches across Australia. In 2010 Melly also began her journey in fabric design and has released seven fabric collections since then.

Melly takes inspiration from her two young children, childhood memories, the beauty of nature and her love of fun and colour. Visit Melly's website to see more of her fun designs at www.mellyandme.com.

Acknowledgements

As always, I feel a need to give thanks to those in my life who continually inspire, motivate and encourage me. Firstly, to my very own 'Super Scotty' who continually believes in and encourages me in everything I put my hand to – love you.

Secondly, to my gorgeous children who are my test subjects and always tell me when something is 'awesome!'.

And lastly, but most importantly, to all of the Melly & me fans out there that send me ideas and encouragement, share their work with me and constantly bring smiles to my day!

This book wouldn't be nearly as fabulous without my trusty test sewers: Christina MacNeil (legend status tester!), Joanna Austin and Isla Chambers. Thank you girls – you have been such an amazing help and encouragement.

Suppliers

Australia

Melly & Me
www.mellyandme.com
mellyandme@bigpond.com

Under the Mulberry Tree
www.underthemulberrytree.com

The Oz Material Girls
www.theozmaterialgirls.com

Fabric Patch
www.fabricpatch.com.au

Patchwork with Gail B
www.patchworkwithgailb.com

Creative Abundance
www.creativeabundance.com.au

USA

Quilting Adventures
www.quiltingadventures.com

Pine Needles
www.pineneedlesonline.com

Heartsong Quilts
www.heartsongquilts.com

Strawberry Patches
www.strawberry-patches.com

Daisy Cottage Quilting
www.daisycottagequilting.com

UK

Hulu Crafts
www.hulacrafts.co.uk

Prints to Polka Dots
www.printstopolkadots.co.uk

Stitch Craft Create
www.stitchcraftcreate.co.uk

The Fat Quarters
www.thefatquarters.co.uk

Sew Hot
www.sewhot.co.uk

Index

appliqué 6, 7, 14, 17, 20–1, 26–7, 47, 55–6, 70, 73, 76
Archie the Alien 8–11, 12, 79

backstitch 76
blanket stitch 76
buttons 7

chain stitch 77
crowns 75
cutting equipment 6

Dougal the Dragon 60–7, 83–5

equipment 6–7

fabrics 7
felts 7
Fifi the Fairy 44–51, 88–9
fusible fleece 7
fusible webbing 7

gaps, closing 77

hand sewing techniques 76–7

ironing 7

knots, sinking 77

ladder stitch 77

machine sewing techniques 76
materials 6–7
Mili and Milo 7, 18–23, 81
Molly the Mermaid 24–9, 82

needles 6

parts, attaching 77
Princess Penelope 68–75, 92–3

ric-rac 16, 22, 28, 38, 41, 60, 62–3, 70–1

Rufus the Robot 30–7, 93
running stitch 76

satin stitch 76
sewing machines 6
sinking a knot 77
skirts 70, 72–3
stitching techniques 76–7
stuffing 7, 78
Super Scotty 52–9, 90–1

threads 6, 7

Unicorn, Yumi the 38–43, 86–7
Unidentified Flying Otis 12–17, 80

whip stitch 77
wings 44–5, 48, 60, 62, 65

Yumi the Unicorn 38–43, 86–7

A DAVID & CHARLES BOOK
© F&W Media International, Ltd 2015

David & Charles is an imprint of F&W Media International, Ltd
Brunel House, Forde Close, Newton Abbot, TQ12 4PU, UK

F&W Media International, Ltd is a subsidiary of F+W Media, Inc
10151 Carver Road, Suite #200, Blue Ash, OH 45242, USA

Text and Designs © Melanie McNeice 2015
Layout and Photography © F&W Media International, Ltd 2015

First published in the UK and USA in 2015

Melanie McNeice has asserted her right to be identified as author of this work in accordance with the
Copyright, Designs and Patents Act, 1988.

A catalogue record for this book is available from the British Library.

ISBN-13: 978-1-4463-0600-0 paperback
ISBN-10: 14463-0600-3 paperback

ISBN-13: 978-1-4463-7263-0 PDF
ISBN-10: 1-4463-7263-4 PDF

ISBN-13: 978-1-4463-7262-3 EPUB
ISBN-10: 1-4463-7262-6 EPUB

Printed in China by RR Donnelley for:
F&W Media International, Ltd
Brunel House, Forde Close, Newton Abbot, TQ12 4PU, UK

10 9 8 7 6 5 4 3 2 1

Acquisitions Editor: Sarah Callard
Managing Editor: Honor Head
Project Editor: Cheryl Brown
Designer: Mia Farrant
Photographer: Jason Jenkins
Production Controller: Beverley Richardson

F+W Media publishes high quality books on a wide range of subjects.
For more great book ideas visit: www.stitchcraftcreate.co.uk
Layout of the digital edition of this book may vary depending on reader hardware and display settings.